# The Armour of Light

## UNLOCKING THE MYSTERY OF DIVINE WARFARE

Anthony Mwangi

Crony Trading Ltd

Copyright © 2025 Anthony Mwangi All rights reserved.

No part of this book may be reproduced, stored in a retrieval system, or transmitted, in any form or by any means—electronic, mechanical, photocopying, recording, or otherwise—without prior written permission of the author, except for brief quotations used in reviews or articles.

Scripture quotations, unless otherwise noted, are taken from the Holy Bible, KJV and are used for illustrative purposes only.

Published by Crony Trading Ltd

London, United Kingdom

Cover design and artwork © 2025 Anthony Mwangi.

ISBN: 978-1-918186-00-0

To the One who is the Alpha and the Omega—
the Light before all lights, the Word before all words.

To the faithful saints who stood when the ground shook,
who believed when the heavens were silent,
and who kept the oil burning in their lamps.

To my family and friends,
who prayed, encouraged, and believed in the vision
even when the path seemed hidden.

May every word in these pages point you
to the Armour of God, the Truth that stands forever,
and the Kingdom that cannot be shaken.

— Anthony Mwangi

"For the weapons of our warfare are not carnal,

but mighty through God to the pulling down of strongholds."

**— 2 Corinthians 10:4 (KJV)**

"The armour is not metal,

nor forged by human hands.

It is light, truth, and the breath of God—

clothed upon those who dare to stand."

ANTHONY MWANGI

# Table of Contents

Contents Title Page

Copyright Dedication

Epigraph

Preface

Introduction

Prologue

Foreword

Chapter 1 - The Stand — Clothed for the Courtroom of Zion

Chapter 2 - Know Your Enemy — The Unseen Thrones, Altas, and the Cosmic War of Dominion

Chapter 3 - The Evil Day — Darkness Without the Armour

Chapter 4 - Having Done All, to Stand

Chapter 5 - Having Your Loins Girt About With Truth — The Covenant of Reproduction and the Government of Life

Chapter 6 - The Breastplate of Righteousness

Chapter 7 - Feet Shod with the Preparation of the Gospel of Peace

Chapter 8 - The Shield of Faith — Quenching Every Fiery Dart

Chapter 9 - The Helmet of Salvation – Guarding the Mind in the Day of Battle

Chapter 10 - The Sword of the Spirit – The Word of God

Chapter 11 - The Power of Prayer – The Final Weapon of the Warrior

Chapter 12 - The Mystery of Boldness and Utterance — Unlocking Divine Speech

The Whole Armour of God – KJV Breakdown

Interlude - The Great Casting Down — From Light to Leviathan

Chapter 13 - The Armour of God in the Heavens — The Stars Declare War

Chapter 14 - The Star, the Scroll, and the Crown — Unsealing the Book of Destiny

Chapter 15 - The War Over Zion — Earth, Land, and Body as the Throne of the Holy Spirit

Chapter 16 - The Holy Fire of the Altar — Consuming, Purifying, Empowering

Chapter 17- Strange Fire and Counterfeit Altars — The Spirit of Balaam vs. the Fire of God

Chapter 18 - The Fullness of God's Armour in One Body — Zion's Warrior Awakens

Chapter 19 - Prayer for Nationalisation into the Kingdom of Heaven

About The Author

Books By This Author

Epilogue

Afterword

Acknowledgement

# PREFACE

This book was born from prayer, warfare, and the relentless pursuit of the truth found in Christ. *Oracles of Faith* is not merely a study of **Ephesians 6** or the armour of God; it is a journey into the depths of divine revelation, where Scripture becomes both a sword and a shield in the hands of the believer.

For too long, the armour of God has been treated as a metaphor, a distant teaching reserved for Sunday school illustrations. Yet, it is the living equipment of the saints, the very spiritual covering without which no child of God can stand against the schemes of the enemy. These pages are written for warriors, those who know the battlefield is real, and the stakes eternal.

Here you will find more than doctrine; you will find a call to action. Each chapter unveils a layer of the heavenly armour, exploring not just what it is, but how it is worn, lived, and manifested in daily life. From having your loins girt about with truth to the sword of the Spirit, and the mystery of boldness and utterance, the message is clear: our fight is not against flesh and blood, but against powers, principalities, and the darkness of this present age.

I have seen the cost of walking without armour. I have also witnessed the victory of those fully clothed in it. My prayer is that every word in this book will strengthen your resolve, awaken your spiritual senses, and remind you of who you are in Christ — a royal warrior, a child of light, a bearer of peace, and a witness of the Gospel, also a kingly priest seated in Zion.

Read with an open Bible, a ready heart, and the willingness to put on the full armour of God — daily, completely, and without compromise.

**Anthony Mwangi**
*Servant of Christ, Witness to is Kingdom*

# INTRODUCTION

From the moment God uttered, *"Let us make man in our image"* *(Genesis 1:26),* the battle began. Heaven's declaration shook the unseen realm. The light-bearer, Lucifer, once a glorious vessel of God's Spirit, could not bear the thought of mankind; made a little lower than the angels, being crowned with glory and honour. Pride gave birth to rebellion, rebellion to corruption, and corruption to deception.

What followed was not merely a fall from heaven but the seeding of a counterfeit kingdom. Lucifer became Satan, the adversary, the accuser — and his deception entered the world through the serpent, a vessel once close to mankind. Both were cast down. The serpent became the cursed Leviathan, the Dragon, and Satan, possessing the spirit of Luciferian, became the deceiver who roams the earth seeking whom he may devour.

This is the backdrop to the spiritual war in which every believer stands. It is not fiction. It is not distant history. It is a present, ongoing conflict that reaches into every decision, every temptation, every prayer, and every victory in your life.

The Apostle Paul, writing from prison, gave the church a blueprint for survival and triumph: *Put on the whole armour of God.* Not half. Not some. The whole. This was not poetic flair; it was a soldier's command. Each piece of armour is more than a concept; it is a divine reality that must be worn, guarded, and maintained.

This book will take you through each element of that armour, showing its biblical roots, its spiritual function, and its application in your everyday walk. You will see how the helmet is more than protection; it is the mind of Christ. How the shield is not only a defence; it is the faith that quenches fiery darts before they ever strike. How the sword is not ornamental, it is the Word of God, sharp enough to cut chains, silence lies, and divide truth from error.

And then, there is the mystery of boldness and utterance, the lion-hearted speech that shakes kingdoms and unlocks divine doors. Without this, the armour is worn, but the battle cry is silent. With it, the Gospel is proclaimed, the enemy is pushed back, and God's will advances and the kingdom is here.

The war is real. The stakes are eternal. And the victory belongs to those who stand fully armed in Christ.

**Anthony Mwangi**

# PROLOGUE

## Before Time Began, the War Began

In the halls of eternity, before the first dawn broke over the face of the deep, God spoke a decree that echoed through realms visible and invisible:

> *"Let Us make man in Our image, after Our likeness, and let them have dominion…"*
> *(Genesis 1:26 KJV)*

It was a sentence full of glory, a breath that carried the seed of divine purpose that creation itself would host a being clothed in God's likeness, walking in fellowship with the Most High.

But in the heart of one once called *Lucifer*, the light-bearer, a fracture formed. He had been entrusted as a seed-bearer of light, a vessel of the Holy Spirit's radiance. Yet when he heard the decree of man's creation, jealousy took root. Pride, that ancient poison, whispered, *This glory should be mine.*

The truth-seed departed from him, and what was once light turned to shadow. Corruption overtook his nature. No longer could he bear the holy light; instead, he became a bearer of a false seed, promising what was not his to give.

Finding a vessel close to Eve, he entered the serpent, whose nearness became his snare. There, rebellion conceived deception. From this unholy union, the serpent was cursed and grew into the dragon, and Lucifer, cast down, became Satan — the Accuser, the Deceiver, the Adversary of all who bear God's image.

Two things fell that day:

- The **serpent** — once a vessel of nearness — reduced, cursed Leviathan, the Dragon.
- **Lucifer** — once the light-bearer — now called Satan, the Accuser and the Deceiver.

The earth itself was cursed, for the seed of rebellion had fallen upon it. And from that moment, the war began in full — the unseen battle between the kingdom of light and the kingdom of darkness.

This war has never ceased. It rages in the heavens, upon and in the earth, and in the souls of men. But the end is written: the Dragon shall be cut down, overturned and overturned, until the Rightful King — clothed in the whole armour of God — comes to claim His inheritance.

And in this truth, you and I must stand.

# Foreword

In a world saturated with noise and endless distractions, the whisper of eternal truth often struggles to be heard. *Oracles of Faith* emerges as both a shield and a compass — a work that dares to pierce through the confusion of our age with clarity drawn from the ancient wells of wisdom.

Anthony Mwangi has not merely written a book; he has forged a living scroll of insight, each page carrying the weight of revelation and the fire of conviction. His words do not float idly in the mind; they take root, challenging and transforming the heart.

What you hold in your hands is not just a compilation of thoughts. It is a journey — from the seed of divine light to the towering armour of truth, from the first whispers of rebellion to the final triumph of the Kingdom. Anthony guides you through these truths with both the tenderness of a shepherd and the precision of a warrior.

This is not a book you merely read; it is one you enter. And when you emerge, you will not be the same.

— *Hannah Mwangi*
Author, Teacher, and Servant of the Word

# Chapter 1

## The Stand — Clothed for the Courtroom of Zion

> *"Put on the whole armour of God, that ye may be able to stand against the wiles of the devil."*
> *(Ephesians 6:11, KJV)*

> *"But ye are come unto mount Sion, and unto the city of the living God, the heavenly Jerusalem… and to God the Judge of all…"*
> *(Hebrews 12:22–23, KJV)*

## The Journey Begins: From Child to Heir

The revelation of the full armour of God begins not with warfare, but with **divine order**:

> *"Children, obey your parents in the Lord: for this is right."*
> *(Ephesians 6:1)*

The Word begins with children because **spiritual warfare starts at birth**. We are born again as infants in the Spirit—heirs in waiting. The child is given **ordinances** (commands), which are the law, the precepts, the testimonies, the way of the LORD.

Through obedience, the child is matured by the Word:

- *Word = Light (Psalm 119:105, John 1:1–4)*
- *Light = Life (John 1:4)*

- *Life = Sonship (Romans 8:14–17)*
- *Sonship = Authority (Galatians 4:1–7)*

We mature into sons of God, *kings and priests* (**Revelation 1:6**), seated in heavenly places, ready to wear the full armour of Christ—not to fight for victory, but to stand in the courtroom of victory.

## The Eden Test: Dominion, Family, and the Partner

After the child matures into obedience, we are led into the family test—the **Edenic pattern** returns:

> *"Fathers, provoke not your children...Servants, obey your masters...do the will of God from the heart."*
> *(Ephesians 6:4–6)*

This stage tests the **faithfulness of the heart**, through intimacy, family, and work. It is where the enemy strikes hardest—because dominion, seed, and inheritance are born here. As Adam was given Eve, and tested in the garden, so every son is tested in intimacy, holiness, and love.

Here is the promise:

> *"Honour thy father and mother...that it may be well with thee, and thou mayest live long on the earth."*
> *(Ephesians 6:2–3)*

This long life is both **spiritual** and **physical**—to remain in the sabbath rest of God, walking in obedience, not defiled by sin, fulfilling the prophetic image of Christ in you.

## The Stand is a Seat

When Paul commanded the saints to "put on the whole armour of God," he was not sending them to war in the wilderness—he was clothing them to **stand in the heavenly courtroom**. The armour is not worn in fear, nor in confusion. It is **priestly, judicial,** and **governing**.

The armour of God is not for *outside* battles. It is not designed for wandering in fear or fighting demons on ground level. The armour is heavenly, priestly, and judicial. It clothes sons—not servants—and positions them in the **courtroom of heaven**, not outside the gates. You are not merely a warrior; you are a **witness**, a **priest**, and a **governor** in the presence of God.

To stand is to **take your place** in the Spirit. This is not a battlefield position but a **legal position in Zion**, the mountain of God, where Christ reigns and judgment is seated. You are not standing on earthly ground—you are standing **in Christ, in the Spirit, in the government of Heaven**.

## The Armour Is for Zion, Not the Wilderness

The armour is not worn by the lost or the afraid. It is not for those wandering in Egypt or begging in the outer courts. It is the covering of **sons and daughters of God** who have ascended in Christ, seated in heavenly places (**Ephesians 2:6**), and now legislate by the Spirit.

Here is where the real war is decided: **Mount Zion**—the place of God's rest, the seat of judgment, and the eternal courtroom of the Spirit.

It is for those who pray as priests, judge as kings, and rule as co-heirs with Christ. This is not merely warfare; this is **governance**.

> "The Lord is our Judge, the Lord is our Lawgiver, the Lord is our King…"
> *(Isaiah 33:22)*

> "And hath made us kings and priests unto God…"
> *(Revelation 1:6)*

## The Sabbath Dimension: Rest in the Courtroom

> "And having done all, to stand."
> **(Ephesians 6:13)**

This stand is **not warfare posture**. It is **government's posture**. You are now at rest not because there's no battle, but because you are now seated in the highest court. Zion is the mountain of rest. And the **Sabbath is the identity of the Spirit**.

The **Sabbath** is more than a day—it is a **dimension**. It is the final resting of all spiritual warfare. The Sabbath is **Zion**, and Zion is the **mind of Christ**, where the judgments of the Lord flow out in peace. You put on the armour not just to fight, but to **stand in rest**, to testify in the courtroom, and to execute the written judgment by the fire of the Spirit.

To stand in full armour is to:

- Be fully matured by the Word
- Be fully governed by the Spirit
- Be covered by the Blood
- Be restored in dominion
- Be seated in Zion
- Be at rest in the Sabbath
- Roar like the Lion of Judah

- Judge like Daniel
- Build like Noah
- Reign like David

To stand clothed in armour is to enter into the **Sabbath of God**. His divine rest, where all works are finished, and His Word governs with power.

> *"This is my rest for ever: here will I dwell; for I have desired it."*
> *(Psalm 132:14)*

> *"With stammering lips… This is the rest… and the refreshing…"*
> *(Isaiah 28:11–12)*

Zion is Sabbath. Zion is Spirit. Zion is the courtroom. It is the dimension where the Spirit of God **rests**, **judges**, and **dwells**. When you are armoured, you are not just defended—you are **positioned** in the seat of His rest and judgment.

# The 7-Dimensional Word Equips the Armour

We will now journey through **each piece of the armour of God**, but not as shallow symbols—we will unlock them through the **7 dimensions of the Word**:

1. **Spiritology** – how it transforms your spirit
2. **Soulogy** – how it aligns your soul
3. **Physiology** – how it governs your body and behaviour
4. **Theology** – the divine truths and names of God revealed
5. **Chronology** – where it sits in God's eternal time plan
6. **Typology** – how it mirrors Old and New Covenant types
7. **Technology** – how it functions in spiritual strategy, fire, and prayer

Each piece is not just armour—each is a **manifestation of Christ**. Each is a legal garment. And every garment is fire-tested by the Holy Spirit to stand in court.

# The Fire of the Spirit: Why the Armour Is Burning

Every piece of the armour is spiritual. It is **fused by the fire of the Holy Spirit**, and you wear it not by flesh, but by Spirit.

> *"Not by might, nor by power, but by my spirit, saith the Lord of hosts." (Zechariah 4:6)*
>
> *"The spirit of judgment and the spirit of burning." (Isaiah 4:4)*

This is why the armour is not physical metal. It is Christ Himself—the **Word** made fire. The Holy Spirit doesn't just fill you—He clothes you in power. He equips you to speak not soft declarations but **judicial verdicts** from heaven's court.

**The Equation of the Word (Psalm 119 Revelation)**

The **Word of God** is the armour. And the Word is not one verse—it is a **living equation**:

Word = Law = Precepts = Light = Testimonies = Judgments = Truth = Righteousness = Mercy = Hope = Salvation = God
(***See Psalm 119***)

This equation proves: to wear the Word is to **wear Christ**. The armour is not metal; it is the **Word made fire**. Christ is the full armour. You cannot separate truth from righteousness, nor peace from salvation—they are one **Person**, one **Spirit**, and one **Body**.

To put on the armour is to **put on Christ** (***Romans 13:14***).

## Servant Proven, Master Revealed

After you pass the stages of child, family, and faithful servant—then the **mystery of the master is revealed**:

> *"And, ye masters, do the same things unto them, forbearing threatening: knowing that your Master also is in heaven..."*
> *(Ephesians 6:9)*

At this stage, you are no longer a servant but an **heir**, seated with Christ in heavenly places (*Ephesians 2:6*). You become a **judge**, a **lawgiver**, a **king-priest** operating from **Mount Zion**, not from the outer courts.

The **Courtroom of Zion** is opened to you.

## From Armour to Roar: Becoming the Lawgiver

Once the armour is on, you are no longer just a soldier. You are the **manifestation of the Lion of Judah**, and you **roar** with power, uttering:

- Justice
- Judgment
- Mercy
- Truth
- Fire

You are clothed in righteousness and filled with the **spirit of burning**. Your words go out not randomly, but **in divine order**, through the Seven Spirits of God (*Isaiah 11:1–5*). Your **mouth becomes a flame**, and your **utterance becomes decree**.

## You Now Function as a Spiritual Judge

When the whole armour is upon you, you are aligned to judge with Christ. Your **identity is prophetic**, your **mind is renewed**, and your **spirit is seated in the inner courtroom**, not the outer court.

> *"The judgment was set, and the books were opened."*
> *(Daniel 7:10)*

> *"Is not my word like as a fire?... and like a hammer?"*
> *(Jeremiah 23:29)*

In this place, your words go out **seven ways**, burning, convicting, building, and establishing God's order in your assigned domain.

## This Is the Courtroom, Not the Battlefield

The real warfare is not on the battlefield of demons—it is in the **courtroom of Mount Zion**, where your words are registered, your garments are spiritual, and your position is eternal.

You are standing by:

- The **power of the blood**
- The **testimony of Jesus**
- The **fire of the Holy Spirit**
- The **rest of the Sabbath**

> *"They overcame him by the blood of the Lamb, and by the word of their testimony…"*
> *(Revelation 12:11)*

> *"For the LORD is our judge, the LORD is our lawgiver, the LORD is our king; he will save us."*
> *(Isaiah 33:22, KJV)*

> *"Out of Zion, the perfection of beauty, God hath shined."*
> *(Psalm 50:2, KJV)*

## The Armoured Son Becomes the Lawgiver

When the whole armour of God is fully upon you, you are not merely **protected**—you are **transformed** into a *throne of judgment*. You become an extension of the Lion of Judah. You no longer echo the noise of panic—you **roar** laws, **utter** verdicts, and **prophesy** with fire.

> *"The spirit of judgment and the spirit of burning"*
> *(Isaiah 4:4)*

> *"He shall not judge after the sight of his eyes... but with righteousness shall he judge the poor..."*
> *(Isaiah 11:3–4)*

This is the fire that was promised in *Isaiah 11 and Isaiah 9*. The **Seven Spirits of God**—Wisdom, Understanding, Counsel, Might, Knowledge, Fear of the LORD, and the Spirit of the LORD—**govern your voice**, sharpen your senses, and **ignite your words into flames**. You are no longer just defending—you are **executing justice** in the gates of heaven.

# Kingship in the Armour: The Spirit of Dominion

*"And hath made us kings and priests unto God and his Father; to him be glory and dominion for ever and ever." (Revelation 1:6)*

Your dominion is restored. When the Holy Spirit clothes you in armour, He doesn't just make you survive battle—He makes you **rule from the courtroom**. Like:

- **David** – with a different spirit and kingly command, governing with justice (*1 Samuel 16:13, Psalm 89:14*)

- **Daniel** – with excellent speech and angelic administration and operating in excellence in Babylon, interpreting mysteries (*Daniel 6:3, Daniel 10:11*)

- **Job** – sitting at the gate as judge, priest, and intercessor; decreeing, interceding, and restoring (*Job 29:7–17*)

- **Noah** – hearing from God in times of judgment and, building an ark of salvation by obedience (*Genesis 6:13–22*)

- **You** – in Christ, now manifesting the **fullness of His image** as declared in *Genesis 1:26* and confirmed in *Psalm 8:5–6*

*"Let us make man in our image… and let them have dominion." (Genesis 1:26)*

*"Thou madest him to have dominion over the works of thy hands…" (Psalm 8:6)*

Now, that image and dominion are restored. The *ark* is your **heart**, built by the Word. The *sword* is your tongue. The *fire* is your spirit.

# The Word That Goes Out as Fire and Returns in Fullness

> *"Is not my word like as a fire? saith the Lord; and like a hammer that breaketh the rock in pieces?"*
> *(Jeremiah 23:29)*

> *"His word goeth forth... it shall not return unto me void"*
> *(Isaiah 55:11)*

When the **armour is full**, the **Word of God comes out of your mouth in 7 streams**—a complete governmental expression of prophetic wisdom, priestly compassion, kingly authority, apostolic order, evangelistic fire, teaching precision, and revelatory sight. The Word *no longer speaks merely to man*—it **executes judgment on thrones**.

This is how we operate as:

- **Officers in the Spirit**
- **Builders of the Ark (the heart)**
- **Executors of Christ's likeness**
- **Reclaimers of Everlasting Dominion**

> *"...greater works than these shall he do; because I go unto my Father."*
> *(John 14:12)*

# The Mystery of the Armour: Replacing Lucifer's Position

> *"How art thou fallen from heaven, O Lucifer, son of the morning!..."*
> *(Isaiah 14:12, KJV)*

Lucifer was once **clothed in light**, full of wisdom and perfect in beauty, walking among the **stones of fire** (*Ezekiel 28:13–14*). But when **iniquity** was found in him, the Spirit **departed** from his body. Though he had been a carrier of the Word, he chose to **rebel against the Spirit**, becoming Satan—the **dark bearer**, the shadow of what he once was.

> *"Thou wast perfect in thy ways... till iniquity was found in thee."* *(Ezekiel 28:15, KJV)*

His body became the container of **darkness**. No longer a vessel of light, Satan is now **disqualified forever** from the place he once held. But God, in His divine mystery, created **man in His image** to take the place that Lucifer lost.

> *"Let us make man in our image... and let them have dominion..."*
> *(Genesis 1:26, KJV)*

Your body is the replacement—the very tabernacle where God now wants to rest. This is why the body must be:

- Full of the Word
- Full of the Spirit
- Full of Fire
- Full of the Blood (doctrine of Christ)

That is the **Armour of Light** (*Romans 13:12*).
Lucifer fell. Man rises. We are now the **Stones of Fire** (*Ezekiel 28:14*).

We do not just wear armour—we are **becoming** the new living weapons of the LORD.

## Your Body Must Bear Light — Or Remain in Rebellion

Our human body is **not holy by default**. It is fallen, fleshly, and vulnerable **just like Lucifer's became** when the Spirit left him. That's why it must be:

- **Crucified with Christ**
- **Filled with the Word**
- **Clothed with armour**
- **Possessed by the Spirit**

If the Word is not **living in your body**, and the Spirit is not **resting on you**, and you're not in sabbath so your body becomes a shell—a throne for rebellion, like Satan's.

But when your body is **armoured in Christ**, filled with fire and truth, you become a **bearer of the light he lost**. You are **replacing Lucifer's place**, not by pride, but by **humble obedience and union with Christ**.

> *"That ye may be blameless and harmless… among whom ye shine as lights in the world; holding forth the word of life…"*
> *(Philippians 2:15–16, KJV)*

## The Full Armour Is Light — Your Restoration to Heaven

> *"The night is far spent, the day is at hand: let us therefore cast off the works of darkness, and let us put on the armour of light."*
> (Romans 13:12, KJV)

The full armour is not just defense. It is **transformation**. It is **your light-body in Christ**—a **heavenly garment** that qualifies you to **walk among the stones of fire**, like Lucifer once did.

But unlike Lucifer, you walk in **humility**, bearing the **Word** not in rebellion, but in **submission** to the Spirit.

> *"He maketh his ministers a flame of fire…"*
> (Hebrews 1:7, KJV)

This is why you must be full of the Word and full of the Spirit to fulfil what Lucifer forfeited. That's why the armour is not physical—it is **Christ, the Light**, and to wear Him is to **bear the light that Satan lost**.

## The Armour is Christ — The Word Made Flesh and Fire

> *"But put ye on the Lord Jesus Christ…"*
> (Romans 13:14, KJV)

> *"Is not my word like as a fire? saith the Lord…"*
> (Jeremiah 23:29, KJV)

The armour is not physical metal. It is **Christ Himself**—the **Word made flesh** and now made **fire** in us. When we "put on the armour of God," we are truly **putting on Christ**. Not symbolically but by living union with Him through **reading**, **obeying**, and **doing the Word**.

> *"Be ye doers of the word, and not hearers only…"*
> (James 1:22)

Every time we read the Word, believe it, and walk it out, the **Word becomes flesh in us;** that is, it manifests in our character, speech, and spirit. That is when the armour becomes real, it fuses with our soul and burns in our spirit.

> *"And the Word was made flesh, and dwelt among us…"*
> (John 1:14)

We wear Christ. We are clothed with the **living Word**. This is why the devil cannot accuse a man truly clothed in the Word; it is Christ that speaks through him.

## Obedience Clothes You in Authority: Judgment Begins with You

> *"If thou wilt walk in my ways, and if thou wilt keep my charge, then thou shalt also judge my house, and shalt also keep my courts…"*
> (Zechariah 3:7, KJV)

This is God's Word to Joshua the high priest. But prophetically, it applies to **every son of God** who walks in the Word. When we obey, when we walk in truth, we are **granted access to the courtroom**, and we begin to **judge the house of God**. This is not human judgment; it is **spiritual legislation** by the Spirit of Truth.

Even more, Paul affirms the dominion of the saints:

> *"Know ye not that we shall judge angels?"*
> (1 Corinthians 6:3, KJV)

This is the courtroom function of sons: to **judge righteously** with Christ, the **true Judge**, by the Spirit of the Word. Not by opinion, but by the **fire of truth**.

# Final Revelation: The Armour Is Your Heavenly Qualification

When you wear Christ fully:

- You carry what Satan lost.
- You walk in the presence of the Spirit again.
- You speak as a son of light.
- You are not just defended—you are **restored** to the seat of glory.
- You are **man crowned with fire**, replacing the fallen cherub.
- You **govern in Zion**, judging what Lucifer defiled.

This is why the Church must rise in the armour—so that the **sons of light may be revealed**, and the **heavenly court restored**, not with angels who fell, but with **men who overcame.**

# The Church Is a Legal Assembly — Not a Crowd

In the Hebrew prophetic sense, the word "**church**" is not a mere gathering of people; it is the **qahal: a people who assemble to legislate;** the **assembly of judges**, **law-knowers**, and **governors**. In Greek, *ekklesia* means **the called-out ruling body**—a governmental structure, not a religious service.

> *"...that thou mayest know how thou oughtest to behave thyself in the house of God, which is the church of the living God, the pillar and ground of the truth."*
> *(1 Timothy 3:15, KJV)*

The true church is not built on entertainment or emotionalism. It is built on **truth**, and it is entrusted with **judging nations**.

- In the **Old Testament**, only **kings judged**.
- In the **New Testament**, every **born-again son clothed in Christ** is a **king and a priest** (***Revelation 1:6***).
- The **true church**, therefore, is made up of those who wear the Word and **judge with the Spirit**.

This is why we are warned in ***1 Peter 4:17***:

> *"For the time is come that judgment must begin at the house of God..."*

You **are** the Church. You are the **sons of God**, with the Word in your mouth like fire, judging angels (***1 Corinthians 6:3***), judging the house of God (***Zechariah 3:7***), and ruling nations (***Revelation 2:26***).

You are now standing in:

- **The Courtroom of Mount Zion**
- Clothed with **the Spirit of Judgment** and **the Spirit of Burning** (***Isaiah 4:4***)

- Anointed by the **Seven Spirits of God** (*Isaiah 11:1–3*)

You are become the **Lion of Judah**. You are no longer running from warfare—you are **roaring laws**, uttering justice, with every word proceeding from your mouth as a **flaming sword**. You are not just attending church.

# Final Charge: You Are the Church — The Government of the Word

You are not just a believer. You are a **lawgiver**, a **king-priest**, and a **judge** in the Spirit. You are clothed with the armour that **burns with truth**, speaks with **verdicts**, and establishes **order** in the chaos of this age.

We wear Christ by the Word. We speak by the Spirit. We judge by obedience. And we **govern from Zion**, where the **fire of God's Sabbath rest** is our courtroom.

> *"Out of Zion, the perfection of beauty, God hath shined."*
> *(Psalm 50:2, KJV)*

> *"The Lord shall send the rod of thy strength out of Zion: rule thou in the midst of thine enemies."*
> *(Psalm 110:2, KJV)*

# Final Declaration of Chapter 1

"I take my place, seated in the heavenly places with Christ Jesus, far above all principalities, powers, thrones, dominions, witchcraft councils, and familiar spirits. I am clothed in the whole armour of God and filled with the fire of the Holy Ghost. I stand in the courtroom, not outside. My body, once fallen, is now the vessel of the Word and temple of the Spirit. I shine in this life as the bearer of what Lucifer lost. I operate from Zion, not confusion. I rest in the Sabbath of His might, not the struggle of my flesh. I roar as the Lion of Judah, clothed in verdicts. I release fire through the Seven Spirits of God. The Lord rebuke every accusation, every tongue that rises in judgment. I testify in the Spirit by the blood of the Lamb and the Word of my testimony" (see Revelation 12:11).

As one made in His image, with dominion restored and destiny fulfilled, I put on the Lord Jesus Christ—I wear the Word like fire, which is the armour of light to replace the darkness Satan brought. I walk in truth, and the Word becomes flesh in me. I obey the voice of the Lord, and I am given authority to judge His house and guard His courts. I am called to judge angels and legislate in the Spirit. I am not part of a crowd, but a member of the holy assembly, the church, the government of God. I stand in Zion. I operate from the rest of God. I do not fight to survive; I reign to establish order. I am the living armour of Christ. I am the voice of His verdicts. I am a lawgiver clothed in glory. I judge not in pride, but in the image of Christ. I am restored to walk among the stones of fire, not as a cherub, but as a son. I reign from Zion. I rule by fire. I am the armour of light.

# Chapter 2

## Know Your Enemy — The Unseen Thrones, Altas, and the Cosmic War of Dominion

*Based on **Ephesians 6:12** & **Ephesians 1:21–23 (KJV)***
*Explained through the 7 Dimensions of the Word of God*

> *"For we wrestle not against flesh and blood, but against principalities, against powers, against the rulers of the darkness of this world, against spiritual wickedness in high places."*
> *— Ephesians 6:12, KJV*

> *"Far above all principality, and power, and might, and dominion, and every name that is named, not only in this world, but also in that which is to come:*
> *And hath put all things under his feet, and gave him to be the head over all things to the church, Which is his body, the fulness of him that filleth all in all."*
> *— Ephesians 1:21-23, KJV*

# INTRODUCTION:

This chapter unveils the **true enemies** of the body of Christ. These are not human beings. These are thrones, fallen angelic realms, dark systems, and altars that war against the divine order of Zion. But thanks be to God — Christ has been exalted far above them all, and **you are seated with Him**, ruling with His authority from the courts of Mount Zion.

Now, we dissect the four-fold evil empire you must overcome:

- **Heavenly Kingdoms** (Apollo, Artemis, Rephan)
- **Sea Kingdoms** (Leviathan, Jezebel, Dagon)
- **Earthly Kingdoms** (Beelzebub, Molech, Azazel)
- **Hell Kingdoms** (Abaddon, Apollyon, Death)

We do so by applying the **7 Dimensions of the Word**:

1. Spiritology
2. Soulogy
3. Physiology
4. Theology
5. Chronology
6. Typology
7. Technology

# PRINCIPALITIES = Fallen Thrones
# (Rebellious Kings in Heavenly Places)

## DIMENSION EXPLANATION

| | |
|---|---|
| **Spiritology** | Thrones that once carried light with Lucifer, but became darkened when Lucifer fell (***Ezekiel 28:14–16***). Now they are inhabited by fallen sons. darkened and oppose Zion. |
| **Soulogy** | War against the soul's inheritance — identity, destiny, and sonship. |
| **Physiology** | Attack **your crown,** the head and your mind (thoughts, mental warfare, prophetic dreams, prophetic sight "visions"). |
| **Theology** | We were meant to rule regions for God, and they were assigned to work for us; they rebelled and now wage **war against Zion** by manipulating cities through false authority. |
| **Chronology** | These spirits are ancient, their thrones predate human kings; they are from the ancient cosmos (***Colossians 1:16***). |
| **Typology** | They are like Pharaoh's magicians or Herod's wise men; Babylon's astrologers and rulers operating through **dark spiritual law**. |
| **Technology** | They use witchcraft altars, digital kingship, AI god-voices, frequency control, and media to rewrite laws, control kings, and program minds. |

**Manifested As:**

- Apollo (false light), Artemis (blood cycles and reproduction), Rephan (false Sabbaths, counterfeit worship).

**Human Agents:**

- Mizimu priests, Freemason kings, witch-doctor clans. *Babylonian Wise Men, astrologers, Chaldeans*

They **replace God's laws with counterfeit ordinances.**

# POWERS = Authorities (Demonic Legal Systems)

## DIMENSION EXPLANATION

| | |
|---|---|
| **Spiritology** | Operate in dark wisdom and perverse counsel; their spirit is anti-Word. Enforcing false laws and satanic decrees. |
| **Soulogy** | They target **conscience**, suppress truth and conviction, and corrupt moral law; distort conscience, and confuse the will. |
| **Physiology** | Manifest in systemic oppression, enforce false health rituals, food defilement, and body binding systems. |
| **Theology** | These are **cosmic judges; they** function like fallen judges executing laws in demonic courts and enforcing Satanic statutes in earthly systems. |
| **Chronology** | Descendants of fallen "watchers" in Genesis and Daniel now they execute demonic decrees. |
| **Typology** | Babylonian counselors who schemed to trap Daniel in law. |
| **Technology** | Control through digital surveillance, courts, police powers, legal AI governance, Biometrics, social credit control, blood law altars. |

## Manifested As:

- *Leviathan (legal twisting),* Jezebel (religious rulership and *witch-law enforcer*), Molech (state and child sacrifice).

## Human Agents:

- Warlords, high-level lawyers in sorcery, the council of witches, *corrupt judges, and sorcerers in political seats.*

# MIGHT = Rulers of the Darkness of this World

This is **darkness that governs** entire systems — education, government, finance, even parts of religion. (Now revealed and redefined by Paul in **Ephesians 6:12**)

These are the Strongmen of Systems – Thrones in Operation

| DIMENSION | EXPLANATION |
|---|---|
| Spiritology | Demonic kings controlling regions, economies, and religions. Strongholds built on deception and ignorance. |
| Soulogy | Darkness = **ignorance, confusion, false religions, spiritual blindness.** Shut down the soul's access to light; replace it with confusion. |
| Physiology | Bind eyes (vision), ears (hearing), feet (paralyse movement); enslave the physical world through structures that bind wombs, dull hearing. |
| Theology | Replace the Word of God with **"another gospel"** with motivational religion. |
| Chronology | Rose to prominence after Babel and intensified after Christ's resurrection; now globalised. |
| Typology | Herod, Nebuchadnezzar, and Pharaoh were shadow-types — human rulers empowered by might. |
| Technology | Social media programming, mind control, government finance portals, Freemason-funded media, demonic education systems, blood-tech, human experimentation. |

**Manifested As:**

- Azazel (*systemic might* and beastly power), Beelzebub (*lord of flies* and ruler of filth), Dagon (religious *corruption*/perversion).

**Human Agents:**

- Enlightenment cults, controlling *False* priests, *media gatekeepers,* globalist elites *UN-aligned global war councils*

# DOMINION = Spiritual Wickedness in High Places (Wicked Altars)

These are the **spiritual courts and altars** of darkness; they are **spiritual technologies,** wicked altars at the high-ranking seated in the heavenlies, and command cities and families.

## DIMENSION EXPLANATION

| | |
|---|---|
| **Spiritology** | These beings preside over blood altars and sacrificial systems. They are priest-kings of Hell, the administrators of fallen altars. |
| **Soulogy** | Create spiritual legal access through ancestral covenants, bloodlines, and defilement. Binding generations through covenant; operate in dreams, soul ties. |
| **Physiology** | Bind generations to curses (infertility and chronic poverty) by creating generational diseases, miscarriages, and deaths. |
| **Theology** | Substitute God's altars with demon thrones—Rephan, Molech, Baal, Artemis. Pervert altars, imitate Yahweh's sacrifices. |
| **Chronology** | They exist **in the heavenly high places** and in city gates, functioning since Cain's offering. |
| **Typology** | Balaam and Balak building 7 altars to curse Israel, the enchanter hired to curse Israel from the mountain tops. |

## DIMENSION EXPLANATION

**Technology**     Altars now function through energy grids, ancestral portals, incantation devices, blood frequency manipulation, satanic AI rituals, and ley lines.

**Manifested As:**

- Abaddon (destroyer), Apollyon (king of the pit), Death (executioner of altars).

**Human Agents:**

- *High-level sorcerers, Chaldean astrologers, enchanters, psychic altars, monitoring spirits,* necromancers, high priest witches, and ancestral mediums.

**Remember:** Isaiah said, *"According to your city, oh Judah, shall your altars be!" (Isaiah 17:8).* These are **city-based high places**, running in opposition to Mount Zion.

# "Every Name That is Named" = Human Agents of the Fallen Kingdoms

These are the **human agents of these realms**, the priests of rebellion.

**Witches, Warlocks, Soothsayers, Diviners, Chaldeans, Magicians, Enchanters.**

**DIMENSION EXPLANATION**

| | |
|---|---|
| **Spiritology** | Human hosts carrying ancient fallen spirits. Channel spirits through incantation, ritual, and possession. |
| **Soulogy** | Trade souls through trauma, seduction (sex), and covenant, even blood pacts. |
| **Physiology** | Infect bodies with poison through drink, or ritual objects, spells and demons. |
| **Theology** | Mix Scripture with tradition, idolatry, necromancy, and sorcery (syncretism). |
| **Chronology** | These existed and operated since Nimrod and continue until now as modern prophets-for-hire (see *Daniel 2:2*). |
| **Typology** | Simon the Sorcerer, Balaam, the wise men of Egypt, the witch of Endor even Jezebel the prophetess. |
| **Technology** | Use internet altars, media spells via video, dream intrusions via voice commands, AI-based idolatry, and blood sample rituals. |

*Named in Daniel 2:2:*

- Magicians, astrologers, sorcerers, Chaldeans
- *Witch-doctors, mizimu priests, necromancers, shamans, "prophets for hire"*

**But you are seated far above all these names.** Whether physical or spiritual, Every name **must bow to the name of Jesus Christ *(Philippians 2:10).***

## YOU ARE SEATED FAR ABOVE

> *Ephesians 1:22–23 (KJV)*
> *"And hath put all things under his feet, and gave him to be the head over all things to the church, which is his body…"*

You are now:

- Seated above these thrones.
- Covered and Equipped with full armour (Word, Fire, Spirit) as Christ, bearing the 7 Spirits of God.
- Wearing Word as Fire, not garments of flesh.
- Positioned and Declaring from the heavenly courtroom of Zion.
- Roaring as the Lion of Judah.
- Wielding the light, not metal.
- Issuing divine verdicts with wisdom, counsel, and power.
- Fighting not for victory but from victory, seated in Zion, the place of final dominion.

**Conclusion: Christ Over All — You in Him**

# This is Not Flesh and Blood Warfare

The armour is not for **carnal conflict**, nor is it a reaction to earthly offence. The warfare described here begins **after** the blood has been applied.

*"We wrestle not against flesh and blood..."*

This means:

- You are no longer walking in sin, which is in the flesh.

- You are now walking **in the Spirit**, and therefore you are a target of **spiritual governments**.

- You are no longer being purified; you are now **being positioned** to judge and overthrow.

You are not just saved; you are **sent**.

# The Structure of Evil: The Four Kingdoms

The enemy is not a feeling. He is a **governmental system**—a rebellious structure of four fallen domains. These are the **principalities, powers, rulers,** and **wicked spirits**.

Each is rooted in **a location, a hierarchy,** and **a dominion**:

## 1. The Heavenly Realm – *Rebellious Thrones*

- **Apollo** – The false sun/light, mimicking Christ's light.
- **Artemis** – The counterfeit spirit of femininity and fertility.
- **Rephan** – Star-worship and planetary witchcraft, including astrology and cosmic rebellion.

These operate in **celestial witchcraft**: they corrupt dreams, visions, and destinies. They tamper with time, seasons, and prophetic alignment.

## 2. The Sea Realm – *Mysteries of Iniquity*

- **Leviathan** – Twisting and prideful spirit, master of accusation and division.
- **Jezebel** – The manipulative, prophetic usurper spirit.
- **Dagon** – Marine idolatry and sexual perversion.

These are **water spirits**, ruling **dreams, sexuality,** and **emotional manipulation**. They mimic the Holy Spirit's flow but bring bondage, not freedom.

## 3. The Earth Realm – *Corrupt Government*

- **Beelzebub** – Lord of flies, filth, and polluted atmospheres.
- **Molech** – Spirit of child sacrifice, abortion, and blood altars.
- **Azazel** – The scapegoat demon—cast into wilderness, working through exile, rejection, and identity corruption.

These are **physical throne holders**, manifesting in systems, leaders, nations, industries, and rituals.

## 4. The Hellish Realm – *The Final Chains*

- **Abaddon** – The destroyer of identities.
- **Apollyon** – The perverter of destiny, orchestrator of spiritual suicide.
- **Death** – Not just the end of life, but the **spirit of separation** from God, reigning in all who refuse Christ.

These are rooted in **Sheol and Tartarus**. They are executioners, finishers of rebellion, and gatekeepers of final death.

# Why We War From Victory, Not For Victory

> "...but against principalities, powers, rulers of the darkness of this world, and spiritual wickedness in high places."

Let's break down this verse dimensionally:

- **Principalities** – *Archē* (Greek): Ancient first-rank beings, fallen thrones.

- **Powers** – *Exousia*: Legal spiritual authorities that govern over territory.

- **Rulers of Darkness** – *Kosmokratōr*: Cosmic rulers over systems of ignorance, perversion, and culture.

- **Spiritual Wickedness in High Places** – *Pneumatika ponērias en epouraniois*: Invisible spirit intelligences operating in the upper spheres of influence (media, religion, politics, false churches).

But note: none of these entities operate outside permission.
That's why **Christ's blood**, **your obedience**, and **the Sabbath seat of Zion** are your legal ground to war.

## The Courtroom of Mount Zion: Where We Stand

You do not fight these enemies on their ground.

You fight:

- From Mount Zion *(Hebrews 12:22)*
- From rest in the Sabbath *(Genesis 2:2–3; Hebrews 4:9–11)*
- With the blood of the Lamb *(Revelation 12:11)*
- By the Spirit of His Might *(Ephesians 6:10)*

You are no longer in the flesh because the *blood redeemed you*. You are no longer under the curse because the *Spirit raised you*. You are no longer a servant, but a *king and priest who judges*.

Therefore:

> *"Having done all, to stand."*
> *(Ephesians 6:13)*

To stand means to **take your seat in Zion**, fully armed with Word, Fire, Blood, and Spirit.

## Roaring as the Lion of Judah: The Verdicts of the Sons

Now, like the Lion of Judah, you:

- Utter judgments *(Isaiah 11:4)*
- Roar like fire *(Jeremiah 23:29)*
- Judge angels *(1 Corinthians 6:3)*
- Replace Lucifer *(Ezekiel 28:14–16)*
- Become stones of fire *(Zechariah 3:2–7; 1 Peter 2:5)*

- **Bear light once lost** *(2 Corinthians 4:6)*

You are no longer reacting—you are *executing divine rulings*.

The courtroom has already been convened.
The enemy has already lost.

You are here to **enforce the verdict** sealed by the blood of the Lamb.

## Seated Above All: The Jurisdiction of Christ in You

> "Far above all principality, and power, and might, and dominion, and every name that is named,
> not only in this world, but also in that which is to come:"
> "And hath put all things under his feet, and gave him to be the head over all things to the church,"
> "Which is his body, the fulness of him that filleth all in all."
> — Ephesians 1:21–23, KJV

These verses **confirm the spiritual geography** of our warfare:

### 1. Far Above All – *"Far above all principality..."*

This phrase reveals that our **warfare begins above the enemy**, not beneath. You do **not climb to victory**—you **stand from it**.

Because Christ is seated **far above**:

- **Principalities** – The rebel thrones in heaven (Apollo, Rephan)
- **Powers** – Demonic legal authorities in systems (Leviathan, Molech)
- **Might & Dominion** – All kingdoms of war, witchcraft, control (Jezebel, Abaddon)
- **Every Name** – This includes every demon, idol, principality, and evil king—named or unnamed.

You are not trying to defeat them.
You are **enforcing their defeat.**

## 2. Not Only in This World, But Also That Which is to Come

This war is **transdispensational**: It transcends time. Christ's throne:

- Reigns in the now
- Rules over the past
- Dominates the age to come

You are operating **from eternity**, not from reaction. That is why the **Sabbath is the seat of warfare**—because the Sabbath is eternal rest, the end from the beginning.

## 3. All Things Under His Feet – The Body's Feet Are His Feet

*"And hath put all things under his feet..."*

Here is the mystery:
When you are **in Christ**, and Christ is **in you**, then **your feet are His feet.**

That means:

- Every demonic throne is **under your authority.**
- Every curse is **beneath your steps.**
- Every evil council is **subject to your command.**

This is why the gospel says, "the God of peace shall bruise Satan under your feet shortly" *(Romans 16:20).*

## 4. He Is the Head Over All – Through the Church

> *"...and gave him to be the head over all things to the church."*

This means the Church is not a building. The Church is:

- The **extension of Christ's government**
- The **Body that carries the throne**
- The **lawgiver on earth** like Judah (***Psalm 60:7***)
- The **mouthpiece of the Ancient of Days** (***Daniel 7:22***)

Your authority comes not from your human strength, but from your **union with the Head**—Christ.


## 5. The Church is His Fullness — You Are the Roaring Voice of Christ

> *"Which is his body, the fullness of him that filleth all in all."*

This is the final blow:

- Christ is the **Head**
- You are His **Body**
- The Body carries the **fullness** of His presence, power, and prophetic judgment.

You are the ones who **utter justice**, who **judge angels**, who **restore Eden**, and who **replace the fallen thrones of Lucifer and his princes**.

You are the **fulfillment of the prophecy**:

> *"Out of Zion shall go forth the law, and the word of the Lord from Jerusalem."*
> *(Isaiah 2:3)*

## Summary: Our Warfare is From the Seat of Christ

You are:

- Seated **far above**
- Warfaring from **Sabbath rest**
- Roaring as **the Lion of Judah**
- Covered in **the full armour (Christ Himself)**
- Enforcing verdicts against the **4 kingdoms of evil**:
    - Heaven: *Rephan, Apollo, Artemis*
    - Sea: *Leviathan, Jezebel, Dagon*
    - Earth: *Molech, Beelzebub, Azazel*
    - Hell: *Abaddon, Apollyon, Death*

You are now wearing fire, not metal.
You are bearing light, not arguments.
You are executing law, not opinion.

This is not religion.
This is dominion.
This is the courtroom of Mount Zion.
This is where **kings arise and rule**.

**Prophetic Word to the Saints:**
*The Body must rise. The Head has already ascended.*
*The feet must now crush. The mouth must now speak.*
*The throne must now rule from the Church.*
*And the Lion must now roar through His sons.*


**Prophetic Declaration:**
*I stand not in fear but in fire.*
*I war not from the flesh but from the courts of Zion.*
*I overcome not by might, but by the Blood, the Word, and the Spirit.*
*The four evil kingdoms fall before the light of Christ in me.*
*I wear the full armour of God.*
*I roar as the Lion of Judah.*
*I judge the thrones of wickedness.*
*I am seated with Christ.*
*I reign from the Sabbath.*
*Amen.*

# Chapter 3

# The Evil Day — Darkness Without the Armour

*Ephesians 6:13 | Amos 5:18–24 | Proverbs 16:4 | Matthew 6:34 | Genesis 2:17*

### INTRODUCTION: THE MYSTERY OF THE EVIL DAY

> "Wherefore take unto you the whole armour of God, that ye may be able to withstand in the evil day..." (*Ephesians 6:13 KJV*)

The "**evil day**" is not just symbolic and a distant apocalyptic event; it is both a personal and **prophetic appointment** in every man and woman's life — the **anti-Sabbath**, the **day of judgment, testing, or exposure**, designed to either:

- Test your armour,
- Expose your nakedness,
- Or demonstrate the **glory** of God in your victory.

It is a spiritual moment in time, often a day of testing, seduction, deception, or visitation — when every human faces the core question: will you stand or will you fall? This is the day where the absence of divine armour will reveal the weakness of flesh.

Just as there is *"the day the Lord has made"* (**Psalm 118:24**) — a day of *rest, light,* and *Sabbath joy* — the **evil day** is the counterfeit. It is the **dark**

**sabbath**, a day of darkness without light, a false day of worship and lawlessness. *Proverbs 16:4* reveals:

> *"The Lord hath made all things for himself: yea, even the wicked for the day of evil."*

## 7-Dimensional Insight into the Evil Day

| Dimension | The Evil Day Defined |
| --- | --- |
| **Spiritology** | A day of spiritual vulnerability when the covering of the Spirit is either tested or absent. |
| **Soulogy** | A day your soul is weighed — decisions from lust, rebellion, or pride determine outcomes. |
| **Physiology** | Manifested often through the **body** — especially in sexual sin, addiction, or sickness. |
| **Theology** | Contrasts the **Sabbath**, which is God's Rest — the Evil Day is **Sabbath profaned**. |
| **Chronology** | An appointed **day of visitation, temptation, or judgment** (*Gen 2:17; Amos 6:3*). |
| **Typology** | Eve's fall, David's Bathsheba moment, Samson's Delilah day — all shadow the **evil day**. |
| **Technology** | Amplified today through media, portals of temptation, and digital environments of lust. |

# THE TWO DAYS CONTRASTED

| The Lord's Day (Sabbath) | The Evil Day |
|---|---|
| *Genesis 2:3* – "God blessed the seventh day…" | *Genesis 2:17* – "In the day thou eatest… thou shalt surely die" |
| *Exodus 31:13* – Sign of God's covenant | *Amos 6:3* – "Ye put far away the evil day…" |
| *Psalm 118:24* – "This is the day the Lord has made…" | *Proverbs 16:4* – "The wicked for the day of evil…" |
| *Hebrews 4:9* – "A rest remains for the people of God" | *Jeremiah 17:27* – "If ye will not hearken to keep the sabbath…" |
| Light (*Psalm 97:11; Isaiah 60:1-2*) | Darkness (*Amos 5:20*) |
| *Revelation 1:10* – "I was in the Spirit on the Lord's Day" | *Matthew 6:34* – "Sufficient unto the day is the evil thereof" |
| Joy, Peace, Rest (*Isaiah 11:10*) | Fear, Temptation, Judgment |
| Righteousness and Holiness | Lawlessness and Lust |
| Life and Blessing (*Psalm 133:3*) | Death and Curses (*Genesis 2:17*) |
| Obedience to the Word | Disobedience to the Word |
| Fruit of the Spirit | Works of Flesh |
| Covenant Marriage (*Hebrews 13:4*) | Unholy Sex (*1 Corinthians 6:18*) |

The **evil day** often visits when one violates covenant — especially sexual purity — echoing back to Adam's fall:

*"In the day that thou eatest thereof thou shalt surely die"*
*(Genesis 2:17)*

It's not just physical death, but spiritual separation — a stripping of glory.

## When Does the Evil Day Occur?

1. **Sex Outside Covenant — *Genesis 2:17, 3:6*:**

The moment Adam and Eve partook of intimacy *outside obedience* (God's commandment), death entered.

*Sex outside marriage is an altar of death.*

2. **Profaning the Sabbath — *Jeremiah 17:27*:**

Refusing rest and holiness opens the gate for fire (judgment).

3. **Departing from the Word — *Matthew 7:26-27*:**

Building without obedience is setting yourself up for the storm — *your evil day*.

4. **Mocking or Ignoring the Prophetic Voice — *Amos 6:3*:**

The "evil day" is delayed, but never denied. Mockers are unarmoured when it arrive.

# THE EVIL DAY AS A PERSONAL TRIAL

Jesus confirms the individual nature of this testing in **Matthew 6:34**:

*"Sufficient unto the day is the evil thereof."*

This implies that every day has its trial. But there is a specific "evil day" designed by the enemy and **permitted** by God to test your obedience, identity, and covering.

*"Thou knewest not the day of thy visitation..."* – Luke 19:44

Just like Job was tested, the "evil day" reveals your preparation. Will you be found armed in the Spirit or naked in the flesh?

**Example Trials of the Evil Day:**

- A temptation to compromise your identity in Christ.
- A seduction into sexual sin outside covenant.
- A betrayal by someone you trusted.
- A spiritual crisis of faith, rest, or hope.

Every human has **a day of visitation**, a **day of testing**, and a **day of judgment**. Some examples:

- **Samson's evil day** — lying in Delilah's lap (*Judges 16:17*).
- **David's evil day** — Bathsheba on the roof (*2 Samuel 11*).
- **Judas' evil day** — betrayal for silver (*Matthew 26:15*).
- **Peter's evil day** — denying Christ three times (*Luke 22:61*).

Yet even on the evil day, **God prepares a way of escape** (*1 Corinthians 10:13*). The difference is who stands clothed, and who is naked.

# AMOS 5:18–24 — THE FALSE EXPECTATION OF THE DAY

> *"Woe unto you that desire the day of the Lord! to what end is it for you? the day of the Lord is darkness, and not light…"*
> *(Amos 5:18 KJV)*

Here, God warns that not everyone looking for His Day is truly ready for it. Many misinterpret their season. Instead of walking in light, they are caught in **religious darkness**, substituting ritual for righteousness.

> *"Take thou away from me the noise of thy songs; for I will not hear… But let judgment run down as waters, and righteousness as a mighty stream"*
> *(Amos 5:23–24)*

**The Evil Day Is Also:**

- A **false sabbath** without obedience
- A **religious day** without righteousness
- A **church day** without the Spirit

Without armour, the "evil day" will devour even the most outwardly religious if their walk is not aligned with righteousness.

# THE ARMOUR MAKES THE DIFFERENCE

> *"Take unto you the whole armour of God…"* (Ephesians 6:13)

This armour is not made of metal — it is Christ Himself. It is the Living Word that becomes your protection in battle. Without the **helmet of salvation**, the enemy strikes your thoughts. Without **having your loins girt about with truth**, you will be seduced by lies and drawn away of to your own lust, and enticed. Then when your lust hath conceived, it bringeth forth sin: and sin, when it is finished with you, bringeth forth death. You will be spiritually dead. This **evil day** exposes those who walk in half-armour or no armour at all.

Those who **walk in flesh** will fail, but those who are **covered in Word, Blood, and Spirit** will stand.

> *"Be sober, be vigilant… your adversary the devil, as a roaring lion…"* 1 Peter 5:8

But **you are also a lion**, the voice of **Judah**, armed with truth, righteousness, faith, salvation, and the Word.

The evil day **does not define you** — it reveals what you're wearing.

# REST IS THE ANTIDOTE TO THE EVIL DAY

The **Sabbath**, the Lord's Day, is not just a weekly observance, it is your **dwelling in the Spirit**. It is where you hide in the Word, rest in Christ, and war from victory.

To survive the evil day:

- **Keep covenant** (especially sexual purity)
- **Remain in the Word** (*Psalm 119:11*)
- **Wear the full armour** daily
- **Take your rest in the Spirit** (*Hebrews 4:9–11*)
- **Pray always in the Holy Ghost** (*Ephesians 6:18*)

# 7-Dimensional Revelation of Amos 5:18–24

| Dimension | Insight |
|---|---|
| Spiritology | The Day of the Lord **without repentance** is not light but judgment. |
| Soulogy | Men run from one trial to another (lion → bear → serpent), **no rest**. |
| Physiology | The body (house) is leaned on, yet still **bitten** — no physical refuge. |
| Theology | **False worship**, noisy religion, and ritualism are **rejected** by God. |
| Chronology | A **prophetic day** approaches where all things fake are exposed. |
| Typology | Like Egypt's darkness (Exodus), this is **thick judgment** to the unjust. |
| Technology | Today, worship through media, false praise, and stage performance is judged. |

**Key Prophetic Truth:**

The *evil day* and the *Day of the Lord* can **both be days of darkness** — **unless** you are **clothed in righteousness and truth**.

Those who merely *desire* the Day of the Lord, but **do not walk in obedience**, will meet a lion (power), a bear (beast kingdom), and a serpent (Satan) — **a full-blown courtroom judgment**.

# Prophetic Symbolism: The Two Days

| Sabbath Day (Holy Day/Sabbath/Zion) | Evil Day (Profane Day/Dark/Babylon) |
|---|---|
| Tree of Life | Tree of Knowledge of Good and Evil |
| Obedience | Rebellion |
| Eden Rest | Eden Judgment |
| Righteous Offspring | Cain Generation |
| A day of rest and ruling (*Hebrews 4:9*) | A day of chaos and judgment (*Amos 5:18–20*) |
| The righteous are hidden (*Zephaniah 2:3*) | The unrepentant are exposed (*Amos 5:21–23*) |
| God receives worship in Spirit and truth (*John 4:24*) | God rejects fleshly performances and rituals |
| Zion sings the new song of the Lamb | Babylon sings loud but in deception and mixture |
| Zion – Dwelling Place | Babylon – Fallen City |
| Rivers of righteousness (*Amos 5:24*) | Waters of judgment, destruction, and delusion |
| Covered in the armour of God | Naked, leaning on the wall, still bitten by the serpent |

| Sabbath Day (Holy Day/Sabbath/Zion) | Evil Day (Profane Day/Dark/Babylon) |
|---|---|
| Christ the Bridegroom | Lust without Covenant |

**Spiritual Warfare Starts Here**

The evil day is a **gateway of either death or dominion**.

- *If you fall*, return, rebuild, re-arm — through the Blood.
- *If you stand*, roar like Judah, legislate like Daniel, walk like Enoch.

**Victory is not escape — it's endurance through obedience.**

# CONCLUSION: THE FLAME THAT DIVIDES

In the vision of the "Evil Day vs. the Lord's Day," a flaming sword separates the realms. The evil day belongs to darkness — the Day of the Lord belongs to light. Those armed with Christ stand on the right side of the sword, clothed in rest, righteousness, and victory.

Your preparation today determines your stance on the evil day.

> *"Having done all, to stand." (Ephesians 6:13)*

**Closing Verse for Meditation**

> *"Take therefore no thought for the morrow: for the morrow shall take thought for the things of itself. Sufficient unto the day is the evil thereof."*
> *– Matthew 6:34*

# Chapter 4

# Having Done All, to Stand

*Ephesians 6:13b | Isaiah 40:8 | Psalm 1:1–3 | Hebrews 4:9–11 | Luke 21:36 | 2 Chronicles 20:17*

> *"…and having done all, to stand."*
> *(Ephesians 6:13 KJV)*

## INTRODUCTION: THE POSTURE OF VICTORY

In the courts of Heaven and the battlefield of the earth, **standing** is not the beginning — it is the result of **finishing**. This **"stand"** is **the posture of one who has passed through fire, kept the Word, worn the armour, and entered rest**. The evil day has come, and you did not fall. You stood.

You did not stand by emotion. You stood by **preparation**.

*"And having done all…"* — implies there was a **doing**, a **warfare**, a **consecration**, and a **resting** before the stance.

# 1. STANDING IN THE COURTROOM OF GOD

This "stand" is not on earth. It is on **Mount Zion**, in the **heavenly courtroom** where Christ intercedes and where verdicts are released (*Hebrews 12:22–24*). To **stand here** is not physical; it is **legal** and **spiritual**. It means you are:

- Clothed with righteousness
- Standing on the Word
- Covered by the Blood
- Full of the Spirit
- Wearing Christ — the full armour

You are no longer appealing — you are declaring. No longer requesting — you are decreeing. You do not fight for victory. **You stand in it.**

> *"Ye shall not need to fight in this battle: set yourselves, stand ye still, and see the salvation of the Lord…"*
> *(2 Chronicles 20:17)*

# 2. STAND = SABBATH = SEAT

To **stand in God** is not to strive — it is to **rest in Him**. This is the mystery of the Sabbath:

- You war six days.
- You stand on the seventh.
- The Spirit rests upon you.
- Zion becomes your courtroom.

Standing is not inactivity. It is **legal placement**. You are standing **because** you are seated (*Ephesians 2:6*), and you are seated **because** you have ceased from your works (*Hebrews 4:10–11*).

This is the posture of kings:

- They **rise to stand** when issuing royal judgment (***1 Kings 3:16–28***).

- Then they **sit** as judges to rule in wisdom (***Psalm 122:5***)

## 3. SEVENFOLD STANDING: 7-DIMENSIONAL POSTURE

Let's break "STAND" down using the 7 Dimensions of the Word of God:

| Dimension | Meaning of "Having Done All, to Stand" |
|---|---|
| **Spiritology** | You are standing in the Spirit, no longer in flesh. Your identity is sealed. You war by revelation, not reaction. |
| **Soulogy** | Your soul is at peace. No fear, no double-mindedness. Your emotions are under Word and Spirit. |
| **Physiology** | Your body is consecrated — no unclean thing. You are temple, altar, and vessel. The armour covers your mortal frame. |
| **Theology** | You know the Word. You believe it. You live it. It has become your standing ground. You're not guessing. |
| **Chronology** | You are in the right season. The evil day came. You were found armed. You did not miss your moment. |
| **Typology** | You are like David with Goliath — not fighting by strength, but by covenant. Like Daniel — standing in Babylon clothed in light. |

| Dimension | Meaning of "Having Done All, to Stand" |
|---|---|
| Technology | You know how to activate and release the Word: prayer, decree, prophetic utterance, Spirit-fire, courtroom language, altar alignment. |

## 4. A KINGDOM STANCE: STANDING AT THE GATE

> *"Blessed is the man that standeth not in the counsel of the ungodly…" (Psalm 1:1)*

In prophetic imagery, "standing at the gate" is symbolic of:

- Ruling authority
- Issuing judgment
- Interceding as watchmen
- Prophetic alignment

The **Proverbs 31** woman (the Bride of Christ) prepares her husband to **sit in the gates** (*Proverbs 31:23*). This is not passive — this is governmental.

> *"Watch ye therefore, and pray always, that ye may be accounted worthy to escape all these things… and to stand before the Son of man."*
> *(Luke 21:36)*

# 5. THE TEST OF STANDING

> *"But he that shall endure unto the end, the same shall be saved."*
> **(Matthew 24:13)**

To stand is to:

- Endure.
- Overcome.
- Finish.
- Be found faithful.

Those who stood were once:

- Children under instruction (***Ephesians 6:1–3***)
- Servants tested in the field (***Ephesians 6:5–8***)
- Soldiers trained in obedience (***Ephesians 6:10–12***)

Now, they are kings in Zion — clothed in full armour — sealed in Spirit — and made immovable by faith.

> *"The grass withereth, the flower fadeth: but the word of our God shall stand forever."*
> **(Isaiah 40:8)**

You are now **one with the Word**. And the Word stands.

# 6. CONCLUSION: YOU STAND WHERE OTHERS FELL

*"Having done all…"*

You have:

- Overcome the evil day.
- Put on the full armour.
- Warred not in flesh, but in Spirit.
- Guarded the covenant.
- Rested in the Word.
- Seated with Christ.
- Arisen as a Lion to judge.

**Now you STAND.**

And your standing makes way for the next chapter: **the Sword of the Spirit and the Fire of the Word**.

# Closing Prayer: Standing in Zion

*Heavenly Father, righteous Judge and eternal King,*
I thank You for the strength to endure and the grace to stand.
You have clothed me in Your armour, You have baptised me in Your Spirit, And You have seated me with Christ in heavenly places.

Today, I stand not by my might, Not by my power, But by Your Spirit.
I take my place on Mount Zion, In the courtroom of justice,
Clothed in the righteousness of Christ, With the full armour of God upon me.

Let every accusation fall.
Let every lying tongue be silenced.
Let every demonic verdict be overturned.
Let the blood of Jesus speak for me!

Father, I declare:
I will not fall.
I will not faint.
I will not fear.
For I am rooted in Your Word, Hidden in Your secret place, And sustained by Your rest.

Now, let Your angels surround me.
Let the fire of the Holy Ghost go before me.
Let my name be written among those who stood.

I enter my Sabbath rest, I rise as a Lion with Your judgment,
And I roar from Zion with Your decree.

For Yours is the Kingdom, The power, and the glory, Forever and ever.
In the name of Jesus Christ,
**I STAND.**

*Amen.*

# Chapter 5

# Having Your Loins Girt About With Truth — The Covenant of Reproduction and the Government of Life

> *"Stand therefore, having your loins girt about with truth..."*
> *(Ephesians 6:14 KJV)*

*The Covenant of Truth, the Power of the Seed, and the Fire of Life - Rebuilding the Covenant Seed*

## 1. Introduction: What Are Loins?

The word *loins* appears frequently in the Bible and always carries weight in both physical and spiritual dimensions. In the ancient Hebrew understanding, **loins refer to the seat of strength, procreation, and inheritance.** The area from which **generations come forth,** representing the **seat of strength, reproductive authority** and where **covenant identity is sealed.**

In Scripture its mean, the **loins** represent the reproductive part of a man's body — the **seat of generational strength,** legacy, and kingship.

> *"...kings shall come out of thy loins."*
> *(Genesis 35:11 KJV)*

> *"...of the fruit of his loins, according to the flesh, he would raise up Christ..."*
> *(Acts 2:30)*

> *"For he was yet in the loins of his father…"*
> *(Hebrews 7:10 KJV)*

The **loins** are where **seed** is carried and not just natural seed, but spiritual **destiny** and **dominion**. It is the place where **godly kings are born**, and where **truth must dwell** in order for that seed to produce righteousness.

Thus, to gird your loins is to prepare your **spiritual reproductive system** — the place where **seeds are planted**, both **physically** and **prophetically**.

When Paul says to "gird your loins with **truth**," he's saying:

- Guard your **generational power**.
- Cover your **intimacy** with the **Word**.
- Let **truth** be the **guide** of your covenant life.

### Truth = Covenant Protection

*Exodus 12:11* – Israel was told to eat the Passover with **loins girded** — signifying covenant readiness.

### Truth = Reproductive Purity

> *"Thou shalt not build the house, but thy son…shall build the house unto my name."*
> *(1 Kings 8:19)*

The **loins** must be submitted to the truth of the Word to produce **a godly seed** (*Malachi 2:15*).

## 2. Truth Is the Seed of Covenant

The **truth** is not just factual; it is **a Person** — Jesus Christ, the Word made flesh (***John 14:6***). When we gird our loins with truth, we are:

- Protecting our **spiritual seed** from corruption (false doctrines, immoral acts).
- Preparing our **spirit-man** to carry the Word like Mary carried Jesus (***Luke 1:31***).
- Securing our legacy through covenant faithfulness.

   *"Wherefore gird up the loins of your mind, be sober..."*
   *(1 Peter 1:13)*

   *"Behold, thou desirest truth in the inward parts: and in the hidden part thou shalt make me to know wisdom."*
   *(Psalm 51:6 KJV)*

To *gird your loins with truth* means to wrap the **reproductive core of your being** in the **Word of God**, so that:

- All that you produce is **true**,
- All that you release is **covenant-aligned**, and
- All that comes from your life is **God-ordained**.

**Truth = Word = Covenant = Seed = Kings**

This is why the **incarnation** happened through a **virgin** (Mary), who conceived by the **Word of God**, the **truth planted in her womb by the Holy Spirit**.

# 3. The Danger of Ungirded Loins: Rome's Fall and Today

*Genesis 3:7* – After sin, Adam and Eve sewed fig leaves to cover their **loins** — their reproductive identity was the first thing affected by **disobedience to truth**.

Hence, truth is the **first armour**, and the **first area of warfare** is around the **loins** because your **bloodline** and **generational legacy** are at stake.

**Examples of Loins in Warfare:**

> **God says, *"Gird up now thy loins like a man."*** 
> **(Job 38:3, 40:7)**

> *"...he was an hairy man, and girt with a girdle of leather about his loins..."*
> *(2 Kings 1:8 KJV)*

In the days of Elijah, this was a **mark of prophetic power**.

Contrast that with Rome: after conquering the world, Rome fell not by war, but by **sexual immorality**. Their **loins were not girded with truth** but **with lust**, leading to **complete moral and generational collapse**. Even today, that empire has not recovered.

The loins are about:

- Strength,
- Identity,
- Reproduction,
- Covenant continuation,
- Prophetic manifestation.

## 4. Loins and the Bloodline of Kings

> *"...God had sworn with an oath to him, that of the fruit of his loins... he would raise up Christ..."*
> *(Acts 2:30 KJV)*

God is deeply concerned with the **fruit of your loins** the **legacy of your life** and the **seed you pass on**. If your loins are not girt with **truth**, then your **lineage becomes corrupted**, and you break covenant like Adam.

> *"...in the day that thou eatest thereof thou shalt surely die."*
> *(Genesis 2:17 KJV)*

That *day* was a **sexual betrayal**, breaking the order of God's truth.

## 5. Prophets and the Girdle

God commanded Jeremiah to wear a **linen girdle** and hide it by the Euphrates. When it was spoiled, God declared:

> *"This evil people, which refuse to hear my words... shall be even as this girdle, which is good for nothing."*
> *(Jeremiah 13:1–11 KJV)*

The girdle was a **prophetic picture of covenant fidelity**. If you're not **girded with truth**, you are **useless** in the kingdom no matter your anointing or office.

## 6. Jesus, the Girded King

> *"...a certain man... whose loins were girded with fine gold of Uphaz."*
> *(Daniel 10:5 KJV)*

> *"...girt about the paps with a golden girdle."*
> *(Revelation 1:13 KJV)*

Jesus is always described **girt** because He is the Word made Flesh, and every part of His being is **truth, covenant, life**.

# 7. The Mercy Seat and the Kiss of Covenant

We now introduce *Psalm 85:10–11 KJV*:

> *"Mercy and truth are met together; righteousness and peace have kissed each other. Truth shall spring out of the earth; and righteousness shall look down from heaven."*

This is the **holy convergence**:

- Truth (girded loins) meets Mercy (the Mercy Seat).
- From this union, **Righteousness and Peace kiss**.

This "kiss" is **covenant conception** — a prophetic **release of life**.

God *breathed into Adam's nostrils* — this divine "kiss" gave **life, Genesis 2:7 KJV**.

The bride asks to be kissed — intimacy with the Word brings forth **life, Song of Solomon**.

So now we say:

**Kiss = Life**

- When God kissed Adam → **man became a living soul**.
- When a man marries and kisses his wife → **life is created**.
- When **Christ kisses His Bride (the Church)** → the **Church becomes fruitful**, because the **Holy Spirit** — the Life Himself — has been released into the Bride.
- When **truth and mercy** meet → **righteousness and peace** kiss → the **government of heaven** is birthed.

This kiss is not lust — it is **divine communion**, a **spiritual transaction** where **the Breath (Spirit) of God** meets the **vessel of covenant** to produce a **godly generation**.

## 8. Loins and the Church

The Church (the Woman) is meant to **receive the seed of truth**, not the **seed of deception**.

- If the **Man** is girt with truth, then the **Seed** he releases into the Church will produce a **kingly generation.**
- But if the loins are **defiled**, then false teaching, false seed, and false children are born.

*"Wherefore gird up the loins of your mind..."*
*(1 Peter 1:13)*

Even the **mental loins** must be girt with **truth** — your thoughts must align with the Spirit of Christ.

## 9. Sexual Purity and Kingdom Authority

Truth in the **loins** speaks directly to the issue of **sexual integrity**.

**Romans fell** through **immorality**, not military defeat.
Their empire was destroyed from the **private parts outward**.

- Girding your loins with truth is to **protect your body**, your seed, your marriage, and your dominion.
- You are preparing your **body to become a throne.**

## 10. The Spiritual Meaning of the Girded Loins

Here is how Scripture explains loins in glory:

- *Ezekiel 1:27* – From the loins upward was fire.
- *Daniel 10:5* – Loins girded with **fine gold**.
- *Revelation 1:13* – Jesus is seen with His loins girded with **a golden girdle**.

**This means:**

Girded loins = Glorified covenant = Fire + Purity + Power
**Closing: Loins, Life, and Legacy**

The **loins girt with truth** is not about metal.
It is about **Christ**, the **Living Word**, the **Spirit of Covenant**, and the **seed of righteousness**.

If your loins are covered with truth:

- Your seed will be holy.
- Your covenant will be preserved.
- Your mind will be strong.
- Your marriage will be blessed.
- Your dominion will be restored.

# 11. Conclusion: The Girded Warrior

You are **not ready for battle** if your **loins are not girt with truth**.

- If your **marriage bed is defiled**, the enemy has access.
- If your **seed is lawless**, your legacy is vulnerable.
- If your **heart is divided**, your lamp will be dim.

But when your **loins are girt with truth**:

- You reproduce **kings** and **prophets**.
- You embody **the law**, not just read it.
- You are **sealed with the Word**, and your children are the **fruit of heaven**.

*"Wherefore gird up the loins of your mind, be sober, and hope to the end…"*
*(1 Peter 1:13 KJV)*

This is **the first piece of armour** because without truth in your **innermost parts**, all the other pieces will fall off.

The armour begins at the **loins** because this is where kings are born. To conquer kingdoms, you must first conquer your loins.

- The *man of God* must keep his seed holy.
- The *woman of God* must prepare her womb for covenant.
- The *church of God* must birth kings — not confusion.

# Closing Prayer for Chapter 5

**Father of Truth, Light and Covenant,**
I present my body to You as a living sacrifice.
Gird my loins with Your with the fire of Your Word — let Your Truth dwell in me richly.
Let my mind be strong and single, full of light.
May I carry godly seed and plant righteousness in covenant purity.
By the power of Your breath, kiss me again —
Give me life, truth, and legacy in Christ.
Let my generations be holy, and my bloodline be sealed in Your truth.
Clothe me, O Lord, with fire in my loins like Ezekiel's vision.
Let mercy and truth meet in me.
Let righteousness and peace kiss in my house.
Let me walk as a king, sealed in covenant, standing in Your armour.
In Jesus' name,
*Amen.*

# Chapter 6

## The Breastplate of Righteousness

*"And having on the breastplate of righteousness."*
*(Ephesians 6:14 KJV)*

The breastplate is not mere armour; it is the covering of the heart, the core of judgment, nourishment, love, and covenant. The Spirit of God reveals that righteousness is not just a behaviour; it is a *dimension*, a garment, a throne, and a manifestation of divine union. This chapter unfolds the *breastplate* as righteousness, judgment, justice, and even the seat of affection.

## 1. The Breastplate in the Spirit (Spiritology)

> *Isaiah 59:17 says:*
> *"For he put on righteousness as a breastplate, and an helmet of salvation upon his head..."*

This is not man putting it on—it is **YHWH** *Himself*. Righteousness is not a human invention—it is divine armour. It protects the **heart** and **spirit**—the seat of decisions, affections, covenants, and even betrayal.

Righteousness is the standard and Spirit that overthrows Babylon. It is the ruling garment of kings and priests in the Spirit. In the Garden, man lost his *righteous covering* and was found *naked*. In the New Covenant, righteousness is restored not just as a covering—but as power, judgment, and intimacy.

## 2. The Breastplate in the Soul (Soulogy)

The breast is the seat of longing and nourishment. In the *Song of Solomon 1:13* and *4:5*, the *breasts* are described as fountains of intimacy and symbols of covenant love.

Righteousness in the soul is the **alignment of affection with truth**, where the Word becomes *milk* (*1 Peter 2:2*) and the breast becomes *the channel of truth and nourishment*. *Isaiah 60:16* says:

> *"Thou shalt also suck the milk of the Gentiles, and shalt suck the breast of kings..."*

This is not only maternal—it is governmental nourishment. Those whose breasts were sanctified in covenant now feed nations through judgment and peace.

But what if the breast becomes polluted? David, the king, once a lion of Judah, ravished the wrong breast (Bathsheba), and from that moment, he lost the sharpness of justice. He could no longer judge his sons, and his throne began to weaken. His body grew cold, and even the virgin brought to warm him stirred no desire in him (*1 Kings 1:1–4*). This is what happens when the *breastplate of righteousness* is corrupted by unrighteous affections.

## 3. The Breastplate in the Body (Physiology)

*Exodus 28:29–30* speaks of the **Breastplate of Judgment** worn by the High Priest, containing the *Urim and Thummim*, lights and perfections. This was worn over the chest, where the **heart beats**. This wasn't symbolic—it was *spiritual anatomy*. The priest carried the tribes of Israel *over his heart*, judging them in righteousness.

When we wear righteousness, our **whole body aligns**, even our **sexual order**, our **digestive system**, our **nervous system**, because **truth has entered the inward parts** (*Psalm 51:6*). The breast is a gate, and judgment flows from the heart (*Luke 18:13*).

Righteousness is not just behavioural, it is physiological when the Word becomes flesh and blood. *Hebrews 5:13–14* says milk is for babes, but strong meat is for those who have their *senses exercised to discern* good and evil.

## 4. The Breastplate in the Law (Theology)

Righteousness is not just a personal attribute—it is **the foundation of God's throne** (*Psalm 89:14*). Every kingdom stands or falls based on righteousness.

In *Job 24:9*, we read:

> "They pluck the fatherless from the breast, and take a pledge of the poor."

This is what Satan's kingdom does: separates the innocent from the righteous breast to feed them poison. But God's kingdom brings the orphan back to the breast of justice.

In *Daniel 2:32*, the image of Babylon had its breast and arms of silver—the **division of heart and judgment**. Righteousness is what **overturns Babylon**, replacing its false judgments with the **holy discernment of the saints**.

## 5. The Breastplate in the Timeline (Chronology)

The breast is always involved in covenant seasons:

- Abraham's seed came from his *loins* and would nurse on the *milk of Sarah*.

- Mary bore Jesus from a holy womb and nursed Him at sanctified breasts.

- Revelation shows the woman clothed with the sun, her **offspring at war** with the dragon (***Rev. 12***).

The **breastplate** is not just a past image—it is a *future weapon*, for the *Bride who will judge the nations* with Christ.

## 6. The Breastplate in Patterns (Typology)

The breastplate is the **seat of covenant judgment** and **nourishment**:

- It is worn by priests (***Exodus 28***).

- It is waved as a **peace offering** (***Leviticus 7:30–34***).

- It is the **seat of the kiss**—where **righteousness and peace** meet (***Psalm 85:10–11***):

*"Mercy and truth are met together; righteousness and peace have kissed each other.*
*Truth shall spring out of the earth; and righteousness shall look down from heaven."*

This is where **Christ kisses His Bride** (***Song of Solomon 1:2***). This kiss is **not carnal**, but *life-giving*, as when God breathed into Adam (***Genesis 2:7***). It was a *kiss of breath*. When Christ kisses the Church, **Holy Spirit (Life)** is released into her and she becomes **fruitful**.

## 7. The Breastplate in Kingdom Dominion (Technology of the Word)

When the breastplate is worn, the *Church becomes governmental*. The Church no longer merely *hears sermons*, but she **feeds nations, utters judgments**, and **executes righteousness** from Zion. This is why *John 21:20* describes the **beloved disciple**—leaning on Jesus' breast—the seat of wisdom and righteous love.

## Conclusion: The Breastplate is the Kiss of Life and Throne of Judgment

We wear righteousness like a breastplate not just to protect our hearts, but to align our **affections, judgments, nourishment**, and **fruitfulness** in God.

We are being **perfected in love and truth**, seated at the **mercy seat**, issuing life, not death. Our chest becomes a place of **pure love, fearless justice**, and **resurrected life**.

**Next Chapter Preview: The Helmet of Salvation**

From the **chest of judgment**, we rise to the **mind of Christ**. We will now examine how the **Helmet of Salvation** guards the **thought gates**, **dream realms**, and **heavenly assignments** of the sons of Zion.

# Closing Prayer for Chapter 6

**Father of Light and Righteousness, clothe me with the Breastplate of Righteousness.**
Guard my heart from strange fire, from unjust love, and from unholy affections.
Let truth spring from within me, and let my soul nurse on Your Word.
Restore my judgments, purify my desires, and establish me as one who walks uprightly.
Let me kiss the Son, and receive the breath of life again.
May Your righteousness and peace kiss within me, and from that kiss let dominion flow.
In Jesus Christ's Name,

Amen.

# Chapter 7

# Feet Shod with the Preparation of the Gospel of Peace

*"And your feet shod with the preparation of the gospel of peace;"*
*(Ephesians 6:15 KJV)*

## 1. Foundation of the Feet in the Word

The armour of God continues downward to the **feet** — a part often overlooked but deeply symbolic. In *Genesis 18:4*, Abraham welcomes heavenly visitors (Yahweh - Jesus Christ Himself) with **foot washing,** saying, **"Let a little water, I pray you, be fetched, and wash your feet, and rest yourselves under the tree."**... establishing the prophetic truth that feet are the entry point to **divine visitation**. Later, in *2 Samuel 11:8*, David tells Uriah to "**wash his feet**," a gesture twisted into a cover-up for adultery — showing how even something pure can be defiled when misused.

Feet in Scripture are **prophetic tools** — for cleansing, conquering, covenant-making, and dominion; it represent our foundation, our walk, and our readiness.

> *Jacob gathers his feet into the bed before giving up the ghost*
> *(Genesis 49:33)*

> *Feet must be shod, ready to move out of Egypt*
> *(Exodus 12:11)*

Feet are **directional gates**; they determine **destiny**. And they also carry us into battle not with swords or vengeance, but with peace. Yet this peace is not passive; it is the authoritative peace of a King who reigns, judges, and crushes the wicked under His feet (***Malachi 4:3; Psalm 47:3***).

This was prophetic, showing how the enemy often attacks our feet — our foundation, our walk — trying to divert the course of destiny.

## 2. The Preparation of the Gospel

What are your feet shod with? Not with dust or vanity but with the **preparation of the gospel of peace**. This gospel is not just about words but **preparation** — a readiness to move, respond, obey, and conquer.

> *"How beautiful are the feet of them that preach the gospel of peace..."*
> *(Romans 10:15)*

The **Gospel of Peace** is good news, but it is also **war news** — peace that passes understanding, and peace that **overthrows chaos**. It is divine order restored through the feet of the saints.

## 3. Feet and Covenant Responsibility

> *"Uncover his feet..."*
> *(Ruth 3:4)*

This intimate gesture wasn't just cultural but **covenantal**. Ruth approached Boaz's feet as a sign of surrender and readiness for **redeemed rest**.

### The Bridegroom's Standard

> *"I have washed my feet; how shall I defile them?"*
> *(Song of Songs 5:3)*

To walk with Christ, the Bride must wash her feet — consecrate her journey, her destiny, her movements. She must prepare herself with the gospel that brings peace to her own soul first, and then peace to the nations.

In contrast, ***Deuteronomy 28:57*** warns of cannibalism — a sign of cursed feet and broken paths. Feet must be aligned to the covenant, or they walk into judgment.

The tenderness of the feet is affected, pointing to how disobedience affects our movement and stability.

## 4. Prophetic Power in the Feet

> *"He set my feet upon a rock, and established my goings."*
> *(Psalm 40:2)*
>
> *"Thou hast delivered my feet from falling."*
> *(Psalm 56:13)*
>
> *"Thy word is a lamp unto my feet."*
> *(Psalm 119:105)*

Feet are not just for standing but for **warfare**, **revelation**, and **transference of authority**.

> *"They pierced my hands and my feet."*
> *(Psalm 22:16)*

Even Christ's crucifixion focused on His feet — where He stood, where He would go, and what He would conquer. The gospel of peace requires that our feet are steady, unshakable, and firmly planted in His truth.

# 5. Dominion from Below: Treading Down

> *"And His feet shall stand in that day upon the Mount of Olives…"*
> *(Zechariah 14:4)*

> *"Feet part iron, part clay — the last kingdom before the stone crushes it"*
> *(Daniel 2:33)*

Christ's return is described in terms of where His feet land. Even the statue of Babylon is judged by what material its feet are made of. That is why we must not walk with "feet of clay" (compromise and mixture) but with feet of iron — prepared in holiness and divine purpose.

From Lamentations to Revelation, we find that **feet carry fire**, judgment, and mercy.

> *"You shall tread down the wicked; they shall be ashes under the soles of your feet."*
> *(Malachi 4:3)*

These precepts reveal that your feet are also weapons. When shod in the gospel of peace, you become a terror to darkness and a vessel of judgment against rebellion.

> *"…the place of the soles of my feet, where I will dwell…"*
> *(Ezekiel 43:7)*

The soles of your feet can carry God's throne when consecrated. Thus, when we walk uprightly, God walks through us.

## 6. Dust on Your Feet or Fire in Your Steps

> *"Shake off the dust of your feet..."*
> *(Matthew 10:14)*

Dust is residue — it represents the **earthly, fleshly,** and **dead**. When Jesus sent His disciples, He taught them to **separate their feet** from defiled houses, defiled cities, and defiled doctrines.

Feet must be **refreshed** with heavenly oil, not soaked in worldly dust.

## 7. The Feet of Peace Are the Feet of Power

> *He began to wash the disciples' feet...*
> *(John 13:5)*

Christ taught that **true greatness is in humble service**. The feet must be cleansed to carry the Word cleanly. A defiled foot means a defiled path. When Mary sat at Jesus' feet, she was positioning herself not just in humility but in **revelation alignment**.

When Jesus washed the disciples' feet. He wasn't just performing an act of love — He was equipping them to walk in His footsteps. He was preparing them to be ministers of peace in a hostile world.

> *"...to guide our feet into the way of peace."*
> *(Luke 1:79)*

Peace is a **pathway**. When your feet are covered in peace, they carry **authority**. Peace isn't absence of conflict — it's **dominion within chaos**.

> *"Mary... sat at Jesus' feet, and heard his word."*
> *(Luke 10:39)*

They are where you touch the earth, and prophetically, where heaven and earth meet in dominion.

## 8. The Gospel of Peace: Dominion Through Sonship

> *"Follow peace with all men... without which no man shall see the Lord."*
> *(Hebrews 12:14)*

Now that our feet are shod, we no longer walk as ordinary men — we walk as **sons**. Your feet carry **power** not just to walk, but to **crush**, **conquer**, and **govern**.

For it is written:

> *"Behold, I give unto you power to tread on serpents and scorpions, and over all the power of the enemy: and nothing shall by any means hurt you."*
> *(Luke 10:19 KJV)*

To preach peace is to announce that the **King reigns**, and that **sons are being revealed**.

> *"How beautiful... are the feet of him that brings good tidings, that publishes peace..."*
> *(Isaiah 52:7)*

> *"How shall they preach except they be sent?..."*
> *(Romans 10:15)*

Your feet carry **power**. Not just to walk, but to *tread down* every serpent of seduction, every scorpion of accusation, every hidden principality of darkness. Your feet are not only for direction — they are for **dominion**.

This is the gospel of peace — *not passive tolerance*, but *active authority*. It is the **good news** that the **Prince of Peace** has crushed Satan under His feet, and we now walk in that **victory**.

• • •

## 9. Dominion of the Feet: The Day of Peace and Power

> *"Behold upon the mountains the feet of him that bringeth good tidings..."*
> (Nahum 1:15)

> *"...they shall bow themselves down at the soles of thy feet..."*
> (Isaiah 60:13–14)

When your feet are shod with the preparation of peace, kings and nations bow before you. You become a portal of divine rest and divine rule.

> *"Our feet shall stand within thy gates, O Jerusalem."*
> (Psalm 122:2)

You are being positioned to stand where Jesus stands. And when He returns, His feet will land upon the Mount of Olives (**Zechariah 14:4**) — and you, being His Body, will be with Him.

## 10. Peacemakers: The Highest Dimension of the Kingdom

> *"Blessed are the peacemakers: for they shall be called the children of God."*
> (Matthew 5:9 KJV)

This is the **seventh and highest beatitude**, the **highest level** of spiritual maturity in the Sermon on the Mount. To be a **peacemaker** is to be a **son** of God — not just a servant, not just a believer — but a **child born of the Word**, a carrier of **Heaven's order** that is walking in the **full power and character** of the Father.

- Peace is not silence.

- Peace is not compromise.

- **Peace is ruling in righteousness.**

Peace is the **last armour on the lower body**, because it's the foundation of spiritual standing. It's the **starting line** of dominion.

The book of Revelation shows that the **true Church** will walk in **peace and dominion**, even in the midst of chaos.

> *"He that hath an ear, let him hear what the Spirit saith unto the churches…"*
> *(Revelation 2–3)*

In the letters to the seven churches, only those who **overcome** and walk in divine order (peace + holiness) are given access to rule with Christ. This gospel of peace is the **qualification** for those who will reign with Him.

# 11. The Gospel of Peace: A Requirement for Glory

> *"Follow peace with all men, and holiness, without which no man shall see the Lord:"*
> *(Hebrews 12:14 KJV)*

This gospel is not optional. If you do not walk in peace — you will not walk into the **glory**. The road to Zion is paved with the gospel of peace, and your feet must be ready.

> *How beautiful… are the feet of him that bringeth good tidings, that publisheth peace…"*
> *(Isaiah 52:7)*

> *"How shall they preach, except they be sent?…"*
> *(Romans 10:15)*

To preach peace is to announce that the **war is over**, that the **King reigns**, and that **sons of God** are being revealed. It is not just a message — it is your identity.

### The Place of His Feet Is Glory

> *"The soles of my feet... where I will dwell among Israel forever."*
> *(Ezekiel 43:7)*

God's **throne** is not in the clouds — it's at the **feet of His body**, the Church. Wherever the soles of our feet tread, **Yahweh sets His Name**.

### Conclusion: Gospel Peace Means Dominion

The gospel is not just forgiveness. It is the government. It is the dominion of peace that Sabbath, not the absence of war. When your feet are shod with preparation, you are armed to walk with purpose, precision, and power.

You are no longer wandering — you are walking. Not sliding — but standing. Not fighting in confusion — but moving in gospel peace.

## Altar Declaration and Closing Prayer

"Lord Jesus, let my feet walk in peace. Let my steps crush darkness.
Make me a peacemaker — not just a hearer of peace but a carrier of divine order.
I will preach, publish, and walk in peace.

I declare: I am a child of God.
I carry the gospel of peace to the ends of the earth.
My feet are holy ground."
*Amen.*


## Prayer to Close Chapter 7

**Lord Jesus,**
Thank You for preparing my feet with the gospel of peace.
Cleanse my path and consecrate my journey.
Let me tread down serpents, trample lies, and crush iniquity underfoot.
May every step I take be in line with Your Kingdom.
Let the soles of my feet be holy ground.
I receive divine shoes — the peace of God which passes understanding, ruling my heart and guiding my movements.
I will go where You send me, and I will not slip nor stumble.
In Jesus Christ' Name.
*Amen.*

# Chapter 8

# The Shield of Faith — Quenching Every Fiery Dart

> *"Above all, taking the shield of faith, wherewith ye shall be able to quench all the fiery darts of the wicked."*
> *(Ephesians 6:16 KJV)*

## THE SHIELD: OUR DEFENSE IN THE SPIRIT

A *shield* is not merely a defensive weapon; it is the *first layer of engagement* against what is thrown at you — accusations, doubt, temptation, deception, fear, lust, depression, curses, and demonic attack. In the physical Roman army, the shield (**Grk. *thureos***) was large and door-shaped, covering the full body when crouched. Spiritually, it represents an active, mobile faith that completely covers your being.

> *"Fear not, Abram: I AM thy shield, and thy exceeding great reward."*
> *(Genesis 15:1)*

This verse reveals the true identity of the shield: *The LORD Himself.* The shield is not a thing but a **Person** — the Word made flesh, the God of faith. The moment Abram chose to believe God's voice (**Genesis 15:6**), he activated his shield. **Faith makes God manifest as your shield.**

# WHAT IS FAITH?

> *"Now faith is the substance of things hoped for, the evidence of things not seen."*
> *(Hebrews 11:1 KJV)*

Faith is **substance**. Not imagination. It is **spiritual materiality**, the seed of the Word. *Isaiah 6:13* calls the **holy seed** the **substance**, meaning faith is the seed of God planted in your spirit. It grows by hearing the Word (***Romans 10:17***), is revealed as fruit of the Spirit (***Galatians 5:22***), and is perfected by **Christ in you** (***Galatians 2:20, Hebrews 12:2***).

## Two Dimensions of Faith:

1. **Faith *in* Jesus** – Believing what He has done for us (***Romans 5:1***).

2. **Faith *of* Jesus** – Living by the same divine trust He walked in (*Galatians 2:20*).

This makes **Faith** not only a gate into salvation, but a **daily life**:

> *"The just shall live by his faith."*
> *(Habakkuk 2:4)*

> *"We walk by faith, not by sight."*
> *(2 Corinthians 5:7)*

# FAITH IS A LAW AND A LIFESTYLE

> *"Where is boasting then? It is excluded. By what law? of works? Nay: but by the law of faith."*
> *(Romans 3:27)*

There is a *law of gravity*. There is a *law of sin and death*. And there is a *law of faith*. When you apply faith, it **governs reality** in your favour. This law lifts you above the curses of the flesh, allowing you to access divine verdicts.

It is by faith that:

- Abraham was counted righteous (**Romans 4:9**)
- Mountains move (**Mark 11:22–24**)
- We are healed (**Matthew 9:22**)
- We overcome the world (**1 John 5:4**)

# THE SHIELD QUENCHES THE FIERY DARTS

> *"...the fiery darts of the wicked."*
> *(Ephesians 6:16)*

These are not just arrows — they are *demonic spiritual attacks*:

- Words of witches and warlocks (**Numbers 23:23**)
- Flaming accusations (**Revelation 12:10**)
- Doubts and whispers ("Did God really say?")
- Lustful imaginations (**2 Corinthians 10:5**)
- Fear and anxiety (**Isaiah 41:10**)
- Invisible arrows of sickness and curses (**Psalm 91:5**)

But the **shield of faith** *quenches* them — putting out the flame before they penetrate the soul.

> *"Take hold of shield and buckler, and stand up for mine help."*
> *(Psalm 35:2)*
>
> *"The LORD is my strength and my shield; my heart trusted in Him, and I am helped..."*
> *(Psalm 28:7)*

## GEOMETRIA & PROPHETIC DEPTH OF FAITH (אָמֵן – AMEN)

In Hebrew, **faith** is rooted in the word אָמֵן (*'amen'*) meaning:

- To confirm
- To support
- To be stable
- To be faithful

**Aleph (א)** = God / Ox / Strength
**Mem (מ)** = Water / Flow / Spirit
**Nun (ן)** = Seed / Life / Eternity

Together, this spells a **seed carried by the strength of God through the flow of the Spirit to produce eternal life**. Faith is divine agreement God's DNA passed through your soul to birth His will on earth.

## THE FIERY SHIELDS OF WAR: SATAN'S STRATEGY

> *"The shield of his mighty men is made red..."*
> (Nahum 2:3)

Red shields symbolised *bloody readiness for war*. But our shield is not red from violence; it is red from **the blood of Christ**.

> *"Prepare the table... anoint the shield."*
> (Isaiah 21:5)

The anointed shield means **consecrated defence** protected by the Spirit. Any un-anointed shield is vulnerable. A believer must live in **ongoing anointed faith,** word-filled, Spirit-oiled faith.

## THE SHIELD AND THE SWORD ARE ONE IN WAR

> *"Who is like unto thee, O people saved by the LORD, the shield of thy help, and who is the sword of thy excellency!"*
> (Deuteronomy 33:29)

When faith (the shield) is activated, it makes way for the **sword of the Spirit** to strike. Faith draws power from the invisible realm and projects it into the battle zone. You need both: **Shield to block. Sword to attack.**

# THE BURNING QUESTION OF JESUS: WILL I FIND FAITH?

> *"Nevertheless when the Son of man cometh, shall he find faith on the earth?"*
> *(Luke 18:8)*

This is the real test in the last days, not church attendance, not titles, not appearances, but **true, burning, active, tested, God-given faith**. Jesus is searching for **His reflection**, and that is a people who have His *faith*.

# THE PRAYER OF FAITH: YOUR SHIELD IN ACTION

Let us close this chapter with a prayer:

## PRAYER

Father, I take up the shield of faith today — not in my own strength but in the Word of God that cannot lie.

Let every fiery dart sent against me be quenched.
I believe, and I declare, that You are my shield, my reward, and my defence.
Let my faith not be in the wisdom of man but in the power of God.
Teach me to live by faith, walk by faith, fight by faith, and overcome by faith.
Let me never be found without this shield — morning or night.

In Jesus' name,

*Amen.*

# Chapter 9

# The Helmet of Salvation – Guarding the Mind in the Day of Battle

*"He put on righteousness as a breastplate, and an helmet of salvation upon his head..."*
*(Isaiah 59:17 KJV)*
*"Take the helmet of salvation..."*
*(Ephesians 6:17)*

## THEOLOGICAL DIMENSION: WHAT IS A HELMET?

A **helmet** is a protective covering for the **head**, the most vital and strategic part of the body in battle. In the natural, it defends the most vulnerable part of a warrior—the brain, the mind, the thoughts, and the face of identity. Spiritually, the helmet represents the **mind of Christ**, the **seal of salvation**, and the **covering of divine identity**. It was first mentioned in Scripture in reference to Goliath, the Philistine:

*"And he had an helmet of brass upon his head..."*
*(1 Samuel 17:5 KJV)*

Goliath's helmet was made of **brass**, a symbol of **judgment** (e.g., altar of brass in the outer court) and hardened pride. But in contrast, the believer's helmet is not metal from the earth, but a spiritual covering from heaven—**salvation** itself, clothed in mercy, righteousness, and the Word of God.

In biblical warfare, it represented **mental security**, identity in battle, and divine covering. Just as a crown sits upon the head to mark a king, the helmet of salvation is the crown of the redeemed. The helmet was the final piece the soldier placed before entering battle, symbolising **completion** and **readiness**.

- In *Genesis 49:18*, the cry of Jacob prophetically opens the door to salvation:
  *"I have waited for thy salvation, O LORD."*

This introduces the idea that **salvation** was anticipated and **wearable**, a hope that guards the mind until fulfilled.

## SPIRITOLOGY: SALVATION IS A PERSON AND A COVERING

- *Exodus 14:13* – "Stand still and see the salvation of the LORD…"
- *Exodus 15:2* – "The LORD is become my salvation…"

These verses show that salvation is **not a concept**, but **a person**. Yahweh Himself in action. When we put on the helmet of salvation, we're putting on the **mind of Christ**, who is our salvation (*1 Corinthians 2:16, Isaiah 12:2*).

The first mention of salvation in the Bible appears in:

> **"I have waited for thy salvation, O Lord."**
> **(Genesis 49:18 KJV)**

Salvation here is prophetic—it is something hoped for, longed for, and awaited. This reveals that salvation is not only a past event or present possession—it is also **a future hope**, **a Person**, and **a covering**.

Salvation comes in many forms throughout Scripture:

- The Horn of Salvation (*Psalm 18:2*)
- The Shield of Salvation (*2 Samuel 22:36*)
- The Tower of Salvation (*2 Samuel 22:51*)
- The Rock of Salvation (*Deuteronomy 32:15*)
- Clothed in Salvation (*2 Chronicles 6:41*)

**Jesus Is Salvation**

> *"The Lord is my strength and song, and He is become my salvation..." (Exodus 15:2)*

The name **Yeshua (Jesus)** literally means **"salvation"** in Hebrew. Thus, when we put on the **helmet of salvation**, we are truly putting on the **mind of Jesus Christ**, the thoughts of the anointed King, and the wisdom from above. This helmet transforms the battlefield of our thoughts and protects us from deception, confusion, and fear.

> *"We have a strong city; salvation will God appoint for walls and bulwarks." (Isaiah 26:1)*

Salvation is described as **walls**—boundaries and protections for the city of God, the soul, and the community of faith.

To wear salvation as a helmet is to wear **Christ's finished work** as a protective identity over your thoughts.

To put on the helmet of salvation is to **put on the mind of Christ** (*1 Corinthians 2:16*).

This is the **complete reversal** of Goliath's helmet — we do not rely on flesh, but on God's Spirit.

> *"Let this mind be in you, which was also in Christ Jesus." (Philippians 2:5)*

The Helmet of Salvation means:

- You are governed by **Christ's mind**.
- Your thoughts are **anointed**, **guarded**, and **disciplined**.
- You live by **heaven's logic**, not the world's fear.

## SOULOGY: THE BATTLEFIELD OF THE MIND

The **helmet covers the mind**, and the mind is where most spiritual battles begin. That's why *Philippians 2:5* says:

*"Let this mind be in you, which was also in Christ Jesus."*

- Salvation **renews the mind**.
- Salvation **guards thoughts** from accusation.
- Salvation **secures your identity** as a son of God.
- Salvation **protects your memory and imagination** from distortion.

*"Wisdom and knowledge shall be the stability of thy times, and strength of salvation…"*
*(Isaiah 33:6)*

The helmet stabilises your thoughts, grants perspective in trial, and brings peace under fire.

## PHYSIOLOGY: HEAD AS CONTROL CENTER

The head contains the **brain**—the seat of decision, perception, and interpretation.

- The brain receives **darts of fear, guilt, lust, anger, and confusion.**
- The helmet blocks every **fiery dart** from accessing your **neural gates.**
- **Hebrew thinking** teaches that the forehead is the seat of remembrance and consecration.

To wear the helmet is to **anoint your neural pathways** with the oil of truth.

## TYPOLOGY: SALVATION AS A COVERING IN SCRIPTURE

- *Isaiah 59:17* – Helmet worn by the Lord Himself.
- *2 Chronicles 6:41* – Priests are "clothed with salvation."
- *Psalm 51:12* – "Restore unto me the joy of thy salvation."
- *Isaiah 45:17* – "An everlasting salvation…"

Typologically, the helmet signifies the **crown of victory, restoration,** and **a renewed covenant mind.**

Compare with:

- **Crown of thorns** – Jesus bore the anti-helmet so we could wear the true one.
- **Mark of the beast on forehead** – False identity in the last days.

But those sealed by God (***Revelation 7***) have salvation inscribed in their forehead (identity, mindset, allegiance).

# CHRONOLOGY: SALVATION THROUGH HISTORY

1. ***Genesis 49:18*** – Waiting for it
2. ***Exodus 14–15*** – Salvation manifesting as deliverance
3. ***Judges – Psalms*** – Salvation as strength and song
4. ***Prophets – Isaiah*** – Salvation becomes a future person
5. ***Gospels*** – Jesus *is* salvation
6. ***Acts – Revelation*** – The church wears salvation and preaches it

*"I will place salvation in Zion…"*
(Isaiah 46:13)

The helmet signals the **fulfillment of all history in Christ**.

> *"And he had an helmet of brass upon his head, and he was armed with a coat of mail; and the weight of the coat was five thousand shekels of brass."*
> *(1 Samuel 17:5)*

Goliath's helmet represents the **mind of the flesh**, **pride**, and **carnal power;** man's attempt to protect himself through **self-righteousness and strength.**

But in *Isaiah 59*, God Himself wears a **helmet of salvation**, showing that **true protection is not from the flesh, but from the Spirit.**

# TECHNOLOGY: THE HELMET AS SPIRITUAL SOFTWARE

Think of the helmet as the **divine firewall** installed in your mind:

- **It filters lies** before they become beliefs.
- **It blocks malware** from demonic doctrines.
- **It syncs your thoughts** with heaven's frequency.

You must **intentionally install salvation** through:

- Confession of the Word
- Renewing your mind (*Romans 12:2*)
- Worship and revelation

## Guarding the Mind

The **helmet guards the mind**. This is the battlefield of spiritual warfare:

> *"Be not conformed to this world: but be ye transformed by the renewing of your mind..."*
> *(Romans 12:2)*

The helmet represents **mental renewal, divine wisdom,** and **kingdom alignment** in our thoughts. The unguarded mind becomes a gateway to fear, deception, lust, or pride. But the mind protected by salvation remains sound:

> *"God has not given us the spirit of fear; but of power, and of love, and of a sound mind."*
> *(2 Timothy 1:7)*

## Work Out Your Salvation

Though salvation is a gift, Scripture says:

> *"Work out your own salvation with fear and trembling."*
> *(Philippians 2:12)*

This shows salvation is not merely an event, but a **process**, a **walk**, a **warfare**, and a **daily renewal**. We must take the helmet daily, lest our thoughts become captive to the lies of the enemy.

> *"Take the helmet of salvation..."*
> *(Ephesians 6:17)*

This instruction implies that salvation is something we must **take intentionally**, **put on**, and **keep on**.

## The Mind of Christ

> *"Let this mind be in you, which was also in Christ Jesus..."*
> *(Philippians 2:5)*

The helmet of salvation is the **anointed mind**. It is not carnal, not fleshly, but full of heavenly discernment. The enemy's chief attacks target identity, memory, self-worth, and the hope of glory. But the helmet protects all of these, because it is **covenantal**, sealed by the blood of Jesus.

## The War of the Wicked vs. the Saved Mind

> *"The weapons of our warfare are not carnal, but mighty through God to the pulling down of strong holds; casting down imaginations..."*
> *(2 Corinthians 10:4–5)*

The **fiery darts** of the wicked—temptations, lies, memories of past sins, confusion, shame, and false identities—are aimed at the mind. That's why the helmet is essential. The Word and Spirit together create a **shield and a helmet** that work together to guard both **mind** and **heart**.

## ACTIVATION: GUARDING YOUR MIND DAILY

1. **Declare:** *I wear the helmet of salvation. I have the mind of Christ. No lie can penetrate the finished work of Jesus over me.*

2. **Pray:** Ask the Lord to *restore the joy of His salvation* (**Psalm 51:12**).

3. **Visualise:** God placing His golden helmet on your head—inscribed "Son of God," sealed with peace and truth.

## SPIRITUAL CONTRAST:

| Goliath's Helmet | God's Helmet |
| --- | --- |
| Brass (Judgment, Pride) | Salvation (Grace, Deliverance) |
| Weighed thousands of shekels (burden) | Light yoke of Christ (Matthew 11:30) |
| Failed to protect (Goliath fell) | Cannot fail (God's salvation is eternal) |
| Mind of Flesh | Mind of Christ |

**True victory begins in the mind** — Goliath was defeated by a **stone to the forehead**, the very place the helmet failed him.

## Prophetic Insights

- The **helmet** sits at the top of the armour for a reason—**as your thoughts go, so will your faith, your decisions, and your vision.**

- **Jesus is the mind of salvation**, not just the heart of it. His thoughts toward us are peace (Jeremiah 29:11).

- To **put on the helmet of salvation** is to **take on the divine perspective**, and to **look from above**, not from below.


## FINAL DECLARATION:

I renounce the helmet of Goliath — the mind of pride and judgment.

I receive the helmet of salvation — the mind of Jesus Christ.

My thoughts are sealed, anointed, and protected by the salvation of God.
No deception shall take root.

I wear His victory the helmet of light and am sealed until the day of redemption.
I think His thoughts.
I see as He sees.

*In Jesus' Name."*

*Amen*

# Chapter 10

# The Sword of the Spirit – The Word of God

> *"And take the sword of the Spirit, which is the word of God:"*
> *(Ephesians 6:17 KJV)*

## 1. What Is the Sword?

The sword is not just a weapon—it is the **cutting edge of divine truth**, the **power of God's voice**, and the **judgment of righteousness**. It was first introduced in *Genesis 3:24* as a **flaming sword** in the hands of **Cherubim**, placed at the **East of Eden**:

> *"So he drove out the man; and he placed at the east of the garden of Eden Cherubims, and a flaming sword which turned every way, to keep the way of the tree of life."*
> *(Genesis 3:24)*

This sword represents **judgment, protection, and holiness**. After the fall, the sword became the **guardian of glory**, blocking man's access to life without righteousness. **To return to Eden**, we must first encounter the sword of truth.

## 2. The Sword is the Word

> *"For the word of God is quick, and powerful, and sharper than any twoedged sword..."*
> *(Hebrews 4:12)*

This reveals the **nature of the Word**:

- It is **living** (quick)
- It is **active** (powerful)
- It is **sharper** than any sword
- It **divides soul and spirit**
- It **discerns thoughts and motives**

## Fire and Sword:

The Word of God is also **fire** (*Jeremiah 23:29*) and a **consuming flame**. The sword of the Spirit purifies AND consumes. It convicts and restores. It divides flesh from spirit and burns lies with truth.

## Spiritology:

The **Spirit and the Word are one**—the Word is the sword only **when breathed by the Spirit**. Otherwise, it's just ink and noise. That's why Jesus said:

> *"The words that I speak unto you, they are spirit, and they are life."*
> *(John 6:63)*

## 3. Dual Nature: Word of God and Sword of God

*"The sword of the LORD, and of Gideon."*
*(Judges 7:20)*

The Word must be united; **your word and God's Word must be one.** Victory is not only declaring Scripture but living it in unity with the Spirit. That's when your words carry divine weight.

## 4. Biblical Sword References: Revelation of Fire and Judgment

- *Deuteronomy 32:41–42* – God's glittering sword devours flesh and executes vengeance.

- *Joshua 5:13* – A heavenly warrior with drawn sword meets Joshua.

- *1 Samuel 17:39* – David refused to use a sword he hadn't **proved** we must also prove our sword (Word life).

- *Psalm 149:6* – The sword in the hand and **praise in the mouth** are weapons of warfare.

- *Isaiah 1:20* – If we rebel, we will be **devoured by the sword** for God has spoken it.

- *Revelation 19:15* – The sharp sword **proceeds from Christ's mouth** to smite nations.

# 5. Sword as Knowledge and Mouth

> *"There is that speaketh like the piercings of a sword…"*
> *(Proverbs 12:18)*

The tongue is a sword. Every word is a blade. The **Spirit's sword** is pure, while the **enemy's sword** is slander, lies, and confusion. That's why:

> *"Their tongue is a sharp sword."*
> *(Psalm 57:4)*
>
> *"Who whet their tongue like a sword…"*
> *(Psalm 64:3)*

## Soulogy:

The **Word divides the soul**. It separates:

- **Emotion** from truth
- **Memory** from reality
- **Feelings** from Spirit
- **Religious self** from living Word

This is why many resist it—it exposes and burns.

## 6. The Sword and Zion's Gate

Only those who pass the flaming sword at Eden can re-enter the **Tree of Life**. This means only those who allow the **Word to purify, cut, and align** will enter glory. The sword guards Eden. The sword grants access to Zion.

This is why the Word will be written not on tablets of stone but on **the tablets of the heart**:

> *"I will put my law in their inward parts, and write it in their hearts…"*
> *(Jeremiah 31:33)*

> *"And the measuring line shall go…"*
> *(Jeremiah 31:39)*

The **Word measures** the city. Zion is measured by the **line of truth**, not feelings. The sword **shapes Zion**.

## 7. Prophetic Insight: Lucifer and the Sword

Lucifer, once a bearer of light, fell through corrupted **word** and **light**. He used **word-twisting** to destroy man. But by the **same Word**, we overcome:

> *"They overcame him by the blood of the Lamb, and by the word of their testimony…"*
> *(Revelation 12:11)*

So, the **same sword** that was used to cast man out of Eden is now given to man to **return**.

## 8. Revelation Sword Timeline

| Scripture | Sword Function |
|---|---|
| *Genesis 3:24* | Guards Eden's glory |
| *Psalm 149:6* | Twoedged, combined with praise |
| *Isaiah 1:20* | Devours rebellion |
| *Jeremiah 12:12* | Devours from land to land |
| *Hebrews 4:12* | Divides soul and spirit |
| *Revelation 2:16* | Sword from Christ's mouth |
| *Revelation 19:15* | Smites nations |
| *Revelation 19:21* | Fills the fowls with flesh |

## 9. Fire, Burning, and Divine Measure

> *"Every battle… is with fuel of fire."*
> *(Isaiah 9:5)*

> *"The LORD shall wash away… by the spirit of judgment and the spirit of burning."*
> *(Isaiah 4:4)*

> *"Precept must be upon precept… line upon line…"*
> *(Isaiah 28:10)*

The **Word is a sword**, but also a **ruler**, a **scale**, and a **fire**. It corrects, cuts, cleanses, measures, and ignites. We cannot wear the sword until we eat it. **Jeremiah, John,** and **Ezekiel** all had to **eat the scroll**—it must become **part of us**.

# 10. Sword of the Spirit: The Word on Fire

This is not just logos (written word) but **rhema**—living word, revealed by Spirit, burning with power. This is why **Revelation** describes it as:

> *"A sharp sword that proceeded out of his mouth…"*
> *(Revelation 19:15)*

Christ returns **not with a physical weapon**, but with a **Word that consumes**.

## Declaration: Sword of the Spirit

I take up the Sword of the Spirit.
I speak the Word of God with power.
I divide soul from spirit, lie from truth, emotion from revelation.
I pierce through every darkness with the Word of Light.
I am trained by the Word.
I speak fire.
I speak judgment.
I speak healing.
I speak life.

The sword is in my mouth, and I wield it with obedience.

In Jesus' Name."

*Amen*

# Chapter 11

# The Power of Prayer – The Final Weapon of the Warrior

*"Praying always with all prayer and supplication in the Spirit, and watching thereunto with all perseverance and supplication for all saints."*
*(Ephesians 6:18 KJV)*

## Introduction: The Final Weapon

The armour of God ends not with something worn, but something done the **prayer**. This is the weapon that activates all other armour. The sword becomes alive through prayer. The shield of faith is raised by prayer. Salvation is renewed in the mind through prayer. Prayer is the incense that keeps the fire burning on the altar of your heart.

# 1. What is Prayer? (7 Dimensions of the Word)

| Dimension | Insight |
|---|---|
| **Spiritology** | Prayer is communion with the Holy Spirit — the breath of God in us. |
| **Soulogy** | Aligns the emotions, desires, thoughts, and will to heaven's mind. |
| **Physiology** | Bowing, kneeling, lifting hands — even your body engages, that's worship. |
| **Theology** | Prayer is covenant dialogue — the legal right to appeal to God's mercy. |
| **Chronology** | There are divine timings — like the hour of prayer (***Acts 3:1***). |
| **Typology** | Incense in the temple = prayers of saints (***Revelation 5:8***). |
| **Technology** | Your voice is frequency. Angels respond. Enemies fall. Spirit shifts. |

# 2. Praying Always — Why Without Ceasing?

Jesus said *"men ought always to pray and not faint" (Luke 18:1).* The devil never stops accusing. Therefore, our incense must never stop burning.

David, a king, teaches us prayer is also **governmental** — *2 Samuel 7:27:*

*"Thy servant hath found in his heart to pray this prayer…"*

## 3. Supplication — What Is It?

Supplication is deeper than prayer — it's pleading, interceding, and travailing.

- *1 Kings 8:28* – Prayer + Supplication = Effective Petition
- *2 Chronicles 6:29* – Supplication comes from pain or personal grief.
- *Daniel 9:3* – It includes fasting, sackcloth, ashes = brokenness.

## 4. Thanksgiving in Prayer

*Nehemiah 11:17* introduces *"the thanksgiving in prayer"* gratitude opens heaven.

- Jesus gave thanks before multiplying bread and raising Lazarus.
- *Philippians 4:6* – *"With thanksgiving, let your requests be made known…"*

Thanksgiving is the **entry gate** of answered prayer.

## 5. Pure Prayer

Not all prayer is heard. *Jeremiah 7:16* shows God can refuse prayer.

- *Job 16:17* – *"My prayer is pure."*
- *Isaiah 56:7* – *"My house shall be called a house of prayer…"*
- Unclean lips and unclean hearts = blocked access.

## 6. The Mountain and House of Prayer

God's House = **Mount Zion** = **Altar of Prayer**

- *Matthew 21:13, Luke 19:46 – "House of prayer... not a den of thieves."*
- *Isaiah 56:7 – "I will bring them to My holy mountain..."*

To pray is to ascend Zion. It is priestly. It is eternal. It is governmental.

## *7. The Seven Altars of Prayer*

1. **Altar of Heart & Character** – purity of motives (***Psalm 51***)
2. **Altar of Family** – priesthood over your bloodline (***Job 1:5***)
3. **Altar of the Enemy** – spiritual warfare & decrees (***Psalm 35***)
4. **Altar of Deliverance** – breaking chains (***Isaiah 58***)
5. **Altar of Grace** – receiving empowerment (***Hebrews 4:16***)
6. **Altar of Love** – communion with Abba (***Romans 5:5***)
7. **Altar of the Cross** – dying daily (***Luke 9:23***)

These altars are the courts of heaven's temple, the trial of every word you utter.

## 8. Watching with Perseverance

To watch is to be alert. To sense in Spirit. To guard spiritual gates. Jesus said: **"Watch and pray lest you enter into temptation." (Matthew 26:41)**

If prayer is your incense, **watching** is your eyes on the fire. Perseverance keeps it burning.

## 9. Prayer for All Saints

Prayer is not selfish. Paul urges we pray:

- For all saints (*Eph. 6:18*)
- For leaders (*1 Timothy 2:1–2*)
- For enemies (*Matthew 5:44*)

Intercession makes you a bridge between heaven and earth.

## 10. Final Revelation: Prayer Is...

- **Seed** (*Job 42:10*) – sown into others, returns as restoration
- **Fire** (*Psalm 141:2*) – keeps the altar of your heart alive
- **Weapon** (*2 Cor. 10:4*) – pulls down strongholds
- **Voice** (*Revelation 8:4*) – brings thunder and judgment from heaven

# ACTIVATION PRAYER

O Lord,
I stand clothed with Your armour.
Ignite my altar with prayer.
Let every altar in me be purified.
Make me a man/woman of incense.
Teach me to pray always, in all seasons.
Let my voice rise like thunder and my tears rise like fire.
I take my place among the watchers.
May my prayers pierce the heavens and break chains on earth.

In Jesus' name,

*Amen*

# Chapter 12

# The Mystery of Boldness and Utterance — Unlocking Divine Speech

*"And for me, that utterance may be given unto me, that I may open my mouth boldly, to make known the mystery of the gospel."*
*(Ephesians 6:19 KJV)*

## Boldness Like the Lion of Judah

This chapter unveils the final spiritual weapon in the armour of God: **utterance** clothed in **boldness**, the fire-breath of the Lion of Judah. It is the *mouthpiece of heaven*, where divine speech is released through yielded vessels.

When Paul prayed for bold utterance, he was not just asking for natural courage. He was praying for a *divine enablement* — the *unction* to speak the mysteries of Christ without fear or shame. This gift is not mere eloquence; it is the **sword of speech**, forged in fire, birthed in prayer, and carried in the breath of the Holy Spirit.

## The Spirit of Utterance: Divine Fire on the Tongue

> *"And they were all filled with the Holy Ghost, and began to speak with other tongues, as the Spirit gave them utterance."*
> *Acts 2:4 (KJV)*

The Holy Ghost ignites the tongue with fire when He fills a believer. At Pentecost, tongues became the evidence of heaven's language flowing through man. **Utterance** here is *not learned language*, but divine syllables filled with the mind and will of God.

## Utterance and Knowledge: The Twin Flow of Wisdom

> *"...ye are enriched by him, in all utterance, and in all knowledge."*
> *(1 Corinthians 1:5)*

Utterance is one of the signs of divine enrichment. When heaven fills your mouth, it also fills your mind for, the mouth speaks from the overflow of the heart. This is **speech that flows from divine insight,** word seasoned by Spirit, grounded in truth.

*2 Corinthians 8:7* shows that utterance is a **grace** we must abound in.

# Boldness: The Spirit's Courage to Speak

> *"...they spake the word of God with boldness."*
> *(Acts 4:31)*

This boldness is not arrogance or human bravery. It is *parrhēsía* in Greek: divine confidence and fearless proclamation. This is the **lion's roar** in the gospel messenger. It is the courage that *shakes buildings*, *silences kings*, and *saves souls*.

> *"In whom we have boldness and access with confidence by the faith of him."*
> *(Ephesians 3:12)*

**Utterance + Boldness = Access.** When we speak boldly under the Holy Spirit's utterance, the gates of heaven *open*, and the veil of man's heart *tears*.

# Word Dimensions of Boldness and Utterance (7D View)

Let us apply the **7 Dimensions of the Word** to these divine tools:

| Dimension | Utterance & Boldness Meaning |
|---|---|
| 1. Spiritology | The Spirit speaks *mysteries* (*1 Cor 14:2*), revealing God's heart in unknown tongues. |
| 2. Soulogy | Boldness realigns the soul — crushing fear, awakening courage, and restoring dominion in the soul. |
| 3. Physiology | Tongues, voice, and breath become **portals of heaven**, physically proclaiming divine will. |
| 4. Theology | Utterance is prophetic speech carrying doctrine, reproof, correction, and instruction (*2 Tim 3:16*). |
| 5. Typology | Moses stammered, but God gave him utterance. Peter denied Jesus but was filled with boldness at Pentecost. |
| 6. Chronology | In the end times, **bold utterance** distinguishes true witnesses from false prophets (*Matt 10:19–20*). |
| 7. Technology | Sound (utterance) is frequency — boldness amplifies the **voice of truth** across time and space (*Revelation 14:6*). |

# Doors of Utterance Are Opened Through Prayer

> *"...praying also for us, that God would open unto us a door of utterance..."*
> *(Colossians 4:3)*

Before the mouth opens, the heavens must open. Every true word of God is **preceded by prayer**, *bathed in intimacy*, and *carried by intercession*.

# Mystery of the Gospel = Mystery of Christ

The "mystery" is **Christ in you**, the hope of glory (***Colossians 1:27***). The more you know Him, the more the mouth must roar.

***Ephesians 6:19*** is the culmination of the whole armour. It is the activation code — once you are fully dressed, your mouth is opened to release the decrees of heaven.

# The Boldness of the Final Saints

> *"...that with all boldness... Christ shall be magnified in my body, whether by life or by death."*
> *(Philippians 1:20)*

This final boldness is **unto death**, if need be, and it *magnifies Christ*. Just like the *Lion of Judah*, boldness is not just for defence; it is the weapon of **offence** in the last days.

> *"Herein is our love made perfect, that we may have boldness in the day of judgment..."*
> *(1 John 4:17)*

In the day of judgment, it will be boldness (not silence) that testifies of our union with Him.

# Final Insight: Utterance Is the Seal of the Armour

All six parts of the armour are spiritual, but **utterance is vocal**.
It is the proof that the armour is *active*, the Holy Spirit is *present*, and the Word is *alive* in you.

When the Sword of the Spirit becomes **spoken**,
When the Shield of Faith becomes **proclaimed**,
When the Breastplate of Righteousness becomes **declared**,
When the Helmet of Salvation becomes **testified**,
When the Gospel of Peace becomes **preached**,
When Truth becomes **uttered** —

**Then the war is won through the Word spoken in boldness.**

# The Whole Armour of God – KJV Breakdown

| Armour Piece | | Line Meaning (KJV Context) |
|---|---|---|
| **1. Loins girt about with Truth** | *l. 14* | Truth stabilises and strengthens. Just as a girdle holds a soldier's garments tight for mobility, truth prepares you to stand. Jesus is ***"the way, the truth, and the life" (John 14:6).*** |
| **2. Breastplate of Righteousness** | *l. 14* | Righteousness guards your heart from sin and condemnation. Not your own righteousness, but Christ's (***Isaiah 54:17; Romans 3:22***). |
| **3. Feet shod with the Preparation of the Gospel of Peace** | *l. 15* | Peace with God through Christ gives you stability in battle. ***"How beautiful are the feet of them that preach the gospel" (Romans 10:15).*** |
| **4. Shield of Faith** | *l. 16* | Faith blocks Satan's attacks—fear, doubt, temptation. ***"The just shall live by faith" (Habakkuk 2:4; Hebrews 11).*** |
| **5. Helmet of Salvation** | *l. 17* | Salvation protects your mind. It gives assurance of your eternal identity in Christ and guards against mental attacks (***Romans 8:1***). |
| **6. Sword of the Spirit (The Word of God)** | *l. 17* | The only offensive weapon—God's Word, spoken in the Spirit. Jesus used it to defeat Satan in the wilderness (***Matthew 4:4***). |
| **7. Prayer in the Spirit** | *l. 18* | Prayer empowers all the armour. It keeps you connected to God, alert, and full of perseverance. It's constant communication with the Captain of the Host. |

# Interlude

## The Great Casting Down — From Light to Leviathan

> *"And the great dragon was cast out, that old serpent, called the Devil, and Satan, which deceiveth the whole world..."* (Revelation 12:9 KJV)

### It Began with a Word

The moment God declared:
*"Let us make man in our image..."*
a trembling shook eternity.
Lucifer — once the **seed-bearer**,
the **light-bearer**,
the very **reflection of the Spirit** —
recoiled in jealousy.

He could not bear it.
How could fragile clay be crowned with glory?
How could dust be given dominion?

### The Departure of Light

Lucifer **rejected the Word**,
and so the **seed** — the **light** — the **Spirit**
departed from him.
He became a **corrupted seed**,
a *telabare* — bearer of false light,

offering what was not his to give.
The serpent, once a creature of nearness,
became the host of his lie.

Eve listened.
Evil conceived.
The false word entered flesh.

## The Double Fall

Two were cast down:

- **The Serpent** — once near to man —
  became **Leviathan,**
  twisted and cursed,
  coiling through generations,
  until he became the **Great Dragon.**

- **Lucifer** — once filled with truth —
  became **Satan,**
  the **Deceiver,**
  the **Accuser,**
  the **Dragon of Pride.**

And their fall took root... like a seed.
The rebellion grew — just like a tree.

## The Fig Tree of Satan

Pride grew tall.
The **fig tree** without fruit
stretched toward heaven.

But its roots were deception.
It bore no righteousness.

Jesus cursed the fig tree.
It was a shadow of the system:
religion without Spirit,
form without seed,
light without truth.

And God declared:

> *"I will overturn, overturn, overturn it... Until He comes whose right it is."*
> *(Ezekiel 21:27)*

## The Risen Man

Now has come the one
clothed in **truth**,
armoured in **righteousness**,
burning with **the Spirit**,
speaking with **bold utterance**,
shod with **peace**,
holding **the shield of faith**,
wielding **the sword of the Word**.

The **Rightful Man**
crushes the serpent's head.

He walks where cherubim stood
and reclaims Eden's gate
with a **flaming sword** in hand.

## Prophetic Declaration

- The **dragon** will fall.
- The **serpent's lies** shall be consumed.
- The **fig tree** shall be cut.
- And the **armour-bearer**, the **true image of God**, shall reign with Him forever.

# Chapter 13

# The Armour of God in the Heavens — The Stars Declare War

*"And there appeared a great wonder in heaven; a woman clothed with the sun, and the moon under her feet, and upon her head a crown of twelve stars."*
*(Revelation 12:1 kjv)*

The war did not begin on earth; it began in heaven.

It began the moment God spoke: ***"Let us make man in our image."***

The Word was released — a seed of eternal truth. That utterance became the dividing sword, and the first strike of war in the heavens. Lucifer, the light-bearer, who once held the Holy Spirit's reflection, could not bear the thought of man being crowned with such glory. He was the bearer of light — the seed-bearer — the covering cherub. But when the Word of the Lord declared man as the image of Elohim, pride was conceived in him. The truth-seed left him. The light departed.

He became a corrupted seed.

Lucifer, the former son of the morning, gave a new word — a lie — and found a vessel: the serpent. The serpent was near to Eve, familiar in the garden, likely a creature of honour and proximity. But now, a transference occurred. The word of rebellion was sown. Evil was conceived.

And so two fell:

- **The serpent** — once a vessel of nearness — was reduced, cursed, and transformed into Leviathan, the twisted, the Dragon.
- **Lucifer** — once the light-bearer — became Satan, the Accuser, the Deceiver.

And *"that old serpent, called the Devil and Satan, which deceiveth the whole world,"* was cast down, and with him his fallen stars, angels that rebelled.

This was no simple stumble. This was the descent of corrupted thrones. The heavens were shaken.

The **fig tree**, a prophetic emblem of Satan's earthly system, began to grow. His counterfeit kingdom took root. He used man's flesh as the soil, sin as water, and deception as light. This fig tree — planted by a lie — reached high through kingdoms, empires, religions, and systems.

But **God's Word cannot be undone.**
The fig tree shall be cut down, for the right Man has come — the one clothed in the full armour of God. The Son of Man. The Lion of Judah. The Last Adam.

> *"I will overturn, overturn, overturn it: and it shall be no more, until he come whose right it is; and I will give it him."*
> *(Ezekiel 21:27 kjv)*

## The Stars Declare the War

The next battlefield was the firmament — the stars.

In the heavens, signs were placed — each constellation a divine encryption, a cosmic scroll. Before scripture was ever written in ink, it was scribed in the stars. The **twelve signs** were prophetic parables of the war between the seed of the woman and the seed of the serpent.

> *"The heavens declare the glory of God; and the firmament sheweth his handywork."*
> *(Psalm 19:1 kjv)*

Satan corrupted even this. The stars were hijacked by astrologers and turned into sorcery, horoscopes, and divination. But the righteous see beyond the counterfeit. The stars are witnesses. They speak without voice.

In *Genesis 1:14*, the stars were created *"for signs, and for seasons,"* — the Hebrew word *"moedim"* implies divine appointments.

Even the **wise men** from the east understood this. They followed a star to find the King of kings.

Just as Jesus has a star, so do you.

## Your Star: Heaven's Record of Your Calling

The Book of Psalms unveils a mystery:

> *"He telleth the number of the stars; he calleth them all by their names."*
> *(Psalm 147:4)*

Every destiny has a star. Every saint, an assigned light. But as we saw with Jesus, stars can be **tracked**, **investigated**, and even **attacked** — just like the wise men were watched by Herod, who sought to kill the King.

In spiritual warfare, the **shield of faith** guards our light. The **helmet of salvation** protects our mind from demonic accusations. And the **sword of the Spirit** — the Word of God — strikes down the watchers who monitor our star.

## Prayer and the Rising of the Star

When the saints pray, stars rise.
When the righteous walk in obedience, they shine.
When Christ is formed in you, your star grows brighter.

> *"And they that be wise shall shine as the brightness of the firmament; and they that turn many to righteousness as the stars for ever and ever."*
> *(Daniel 12:3)*

But if your star has been imprisoned, caged in marine altars or bound by sorcery, it must be **redeemed**. The courtroom of heaven must be invoked. The blood of Jesus must speak. Your prayer must pierce the night.

Let every reader now declare:

**"O Lord, arise and fight for my star!
Let the sword of the Spirit go forth and restore my destiny, in Jesus' name!"**

*Amen*

# Chapter 14

## The Star, the Scroll, and the Crown — Unsealing the Book of Destiny

*"Lo, I come: in the volume of the book it is written of me..."*
**(Psalm 40:7) - (cf. Hebrews 10:7)**

*"Then I saw in the right hand of him who sat on the throne a scroll with writing on both sides and sealed with seven seals."*
**(Revelation 5:1)**

Every soul born of God carries a **scroll**, a **star**, and a **crown** — three heavenly symbols of divine purpose:

1. **The Star** is your heavenly identity — your light in the firmament, tied to your assignment and calling.

2. **The Scroll** is the record — the encoded book of your destiny written before the foundation of the world.

3. **The Crown** is your reward — given to those who overcome and finish their course in Christ.

But as with all things holy, these can be contended for, sealed, delayed, or warred against by spiritual powers of darkness. Many destinies remain locked, not because God is unwilling, but because the saints are unaware.

*"My people are destroyed for lack of knowledge..."*
**(Hosea 4:6)**

Let us now journey deeper into this holy triad.

# 1. The Star — Your Light Before God

> *"Those who are wise will shine like the brightness of the heavens, and those who lead many to righteousness, like the stars forever and ever."*
> *(Daniel 12:3)*

The star is not just in the sky — it is in the Spirit.
When Jesus was born, **His star** appeared. (*Matthew 2:2*)
When Joseph dreamed, the **sun, moon, and stars** bowed to him — a sign of spiritual authority.

But the **serpent kingdom also watches stars.**

In *Revelation 12:4*, the Dragon's tail drew one-third of the stars and cast them to the earth — these were the fallen angels, and by type, **destinies diverted.**

Witchcraft, marine altars, and ancestral covenants can monitor or even imprison a person's star.

The solution?

The **blood of Jesus, the sword of the Spirit,** and **heavenly warfare.**

## 2. The Scroll — The Book of Destiny

*"In thy book all my members were written, which in continuance were fashioned, when as yet there was none of them."*
*(Psalm 139:16)*

Before you were born, **your story was written.**
There is a scroll that only the **Lamb** can open — the record of every life, the true manuscript of purpose.

When a person walks in sin, rebellion, or deception, the scroll remains sealed.
When they come into Christ and begin to live by the Spirit, the scroll **begins to open.**

John wept in ***Revelation 5*** because no man could open the scroll. But then he saw the **Lion of Judah** — and **He had prevailed.**

**Only Jesus can unlock your true self.**

Your scroll is not just your ministry — it includes your **timing**, **relationships**, **assignments**, **territories**, and even **mantles** from heaven.

# 3. The Crown — The Reward of Overcoming

> *"Behold, I come quickly: hold that fast which thou hast, that no man take thy crown."*
> *(Revelation 3:11)*

The crown is given **after victory**.
We do not receive it because we are saved, but because we **finished well**.

The Apostle Paul said:

> *"I have fought a good fight, I have finished my course, I have kept the faith: henceforth there is laid up for me a crown…"*
> *(2 Timothy 4:7–8)*

There are different crowns:

- Crown of life — for those who endure trials and love God.
- Crown of righteousness — for those who long for Christ's appearing.
- Crown of glory — for faithful shepherds and leaders.
- Incorruptible crown — for disciplined, self-controlled saints.
- Crown of rejoicing — for soul winners.

But **beware** — your crown can be lost (***Revelation 3:11***).
Stolen by deception, laziness, sin, or compromise.

## The Battle of the Books

In the heavenly courtroom, two books are open:

1. The **Book of Accusation** — held by Satan, the accuser of the brethren.
2. The **Book of Destiny** — held by the Lamb, sealed with righteousness.

Your **star** must agree with your **scroll**,
And your **life** must match the **record** for your **crown** to be secured.

When we pray in the Spirit, we **war for what is written**.

*"Open the book, O Lord. Let what is written of me come to pass."*


## Prophetic Action Point:

Declare with boldness:

**I reject every counterfeit scroll.**
**I renounce every false crown.**
**I call forth my true star, my divine scroll, and the crown of my calling.**
**Let the blood of Jesus speak for me in the courtroom of heaven.**
**I am who God says I am, and I will finish well.**

**In Jesus Christ's Mighty name.** *Amen*

# Chapter 15

## The War Over Zion — Earth, Land, and Body as the Throne of the Holy Spirit

> *"For the Lord hath chosen Zion; He hath desired it for His habitation."*
> *(Psalm 132:13)*
>
> *"This is my rest for ever: here will I dwell; for I have desired it."*
> *(Psalm 132:14)*

From Genesis to Revelation, the **central war** has always been about **Zion** — the throne, the resting place of the **Spirit of God**. Zion is not only a mountain in Israel. It is a prophetic symbol of:

- **The Earth** — the Lord's footstool.
- **The Land (Nations)** — where His kingdom comes.
- **The Body (Man)** — the temple of the Holy Spirit.

## 1. Zion in the Earth: The Place of His Feet

> *"Heaven is my throne, and earth is my footstool."*
> *(Isaiah 66:1)*

When Lucifer fell, he was cast **into the earth** (***Revelation 12:9***).
This earth, originally designed to carry the **glory** and **rest** of God, became defiled by rebellion.
The curse entered. The ground was stained with blood.
But **God did not abandon the earth** — He had a plan of **restoration**.

Through the **seed of the woman**, a **man** would crush the serpent's head (***Genesis 3:15***).
And through this man, the **Spirit of God would once again dwell on the earth** — in **flesh**.

> *"The Word became flesh and dwelt among us..."*
> *(John 1:14)*

## 2. Zion in the Land: The Nations as His Inheritance

> *"Ask of me, and I shall give thee the heathen for thine inheritance..."*
> *(Psalm 2:8)*

The **land** — whether Canaan, Eden, or the nations was always meant to reflect the kingdom of God.

The battle over **territories, regions, and altars** is a battle over **who will rule** in the land: the **Spirit of God** or the **spirit of Satan**.

Just as God chose Israel to be a holy nation, so now He calls every nation to **return to Zion** — the place of His Spirit's rest.

When God's Spirit reigns in a land, there is peace, justice, and harvest. When demons rule, there is chaos, bloodshed, and bondage.

This is why **prayer altars**, **repentance**, and **righteous governance** are not optional — they are spiritual gates that open the land to **Zion's reign**.

## 3. Zion in the Body: Man as God's Resting Place

> *"Know ye not that your body is the temple of the Holy Ghost?"*
> *(1 Corinthians 6:19)*

This is the **deepest layer** of Zion's mystery:
God does not just want to reign in the heavens or in nations — **He wants to reign in YOU.**
You were designed to be His **temple**, His **throne**, His **rest**.

The war over your body is a war over God's throne.

The Holy Spirit left man when Adam sinned.
For 4,000 years, the **Spirit hovered** upon prophets, kings, judges — but never found permanent **rest**.
Until Jesus came.

> *"This is my beloved Son in whom I am well pleased; upon whom the Spirit remains."*
> *(John 1:33)*

And now, through Christ, we are being rebuilt into a **habitation of God through the Spirit** (*Ephesians 2:22*).

## The Three-Domain Sabbath Rest

| Domain | Original Purpose | Defilement Cause | Restoration Plan |
|---|---|---|---|
| Earth | Footstool of God | Lucifer's fall | The Second Adam (Jesus) brings dominion back |
| Land/Nations | Inheritance of the Lord | Idolatry and false altars | Kingdom Intercession, Holy Governance |
| Body | Temple of the Spirit | Sin, rebellion, flesh | Redemption, Purification, Indwelling of the Holy Spirit |

## Zion: The Mind and Heart of God

*"Let this mind be in you which was also in Christ Jesus…" (Philippians 2:5)*

- **Zion is the mind** — the inner altar where God's thoughts dwell.
- **Jerusalem is the heart** — the place of deep spiritual transactions.

When **Zion rules**, your mind is sober, your soul is at peace, and your body becomes a vessel of power. But when **Babylon rules**, confusion, compromise, and rebellion set in.

# The Final Battle: Who Will Sit on the Throne?

> *"...I will return into my house from whence I came out..."*
> *(Matthew 12:44)*

Demons fight for bodies.
The Holy Spirit fights for bodies.
Satan imitates possession — God desires **habitation**.

Your body is the Zion He has chosen.
Will you yield to the Spirit or to the flesh?

## Prophetic Decree:

O Lord, I yield my body, my land, and my earth to be Zion — Your throne of rest.
Let every serpent, every false altar, and every Babylonian gate be overthrown.
Dwell in me, reign in me, rest in me, O Spirit of God, The Spirit of Judgement and Burning.

**In Jesus Christ, Mighty Name**

*Amen*

# Chapter 16

# The Holy Fire of the Altar — Consuming, Purifying, Empowering

*"The fire shall ever be burning upon the altar; it shall never go out."*
*(Leviticus 6:13)*

## Fire: The Signature of God's Presence

Throughout the Scriptures, **fire is never just an element**. It is the **manifestation of God Himself** — His **voice**, His **judgment**, His **purity**, and His **power**.

From the **burning bush** that called Moses (***Exodus 3:2***)
To the **pillar of fire** that led Israel (***Exodus 13:21***)
To the **fire on Mount Sinai** where the Law was given (***Exodus 19:18***)
To the **fire of Pentecost** that sat upon each disciple (***Acts 2:3***)

The altar without fire is just cold stone.
The temple without fire is just empty ritual.
The body without fire is just flesh.

# Three Dimensions of Fire at the Altar

1. **Consuming Fire** – *To destroy what cannot dwell with God.*

*"For our God is a consuming fire."*
*(Hebrews 12:29)*

This is the **fire of judgment**, but also the fire of love.
It burns away every false thing: pride, lust, idols, lies, flesh.
This is the **refiner's fire** (*Malachi 3:2–3*).

You cannot carry God's fire and keep your idols.

2. **Purifying Fire** – *To cleanse the vessel for holy use.*

*"I will turn my hand upon thee, and purely purge away thy dross..."*
*(Isaiah 1:25)*

The altar of your body, your mind, and your spirit must be purged.
You must be **washed in fire** — the fire of His **Word**, the fire of His **Spirit**, the fire of **truth**.

Only clean vessels can carry holy flames.

3. **Empowering Fire** – *To release divine power and utterance.*

*"Ye shall receive power, after that the Holy Ghost is come upon you..."*
*(Acts 1:8)*

The fire of Pentecost was not to entertain. It was to **empower** — for speech, signs, wonders, witness.
Every true revival is born in fire.
Every true voice of God is forged in fire.

## The Fire Must Never Go Out

> *"The fire shall ever be burning upon the altar; it shall never go out."*
> *(Leviticus 6:13)*

This is not just a priestly command — it's a **daily spiritual law**.
The altar of your spirit must **never go cold**.
This fire must be **fed by the Word**, **fueled by prayer**, and **guarded by obedience**.

## Elijah's Fire: A Prophetic Blueprint

> *"Then the fire of the Lord fell..."*
> *(1 Kings 18:38)*

When Elijah repaired the broken altar,
Set the wood in order,
Laid the sacrifice,
And prayed according to the covenant —
**The fire fell.**

This is the pattern for every fire-restoration today:

1. **Repair the altar** (repentance and consecration)
2. **Order the wood** (structure your life around God)
3. **Lay the sacrifice** (present your body — ***Romans 12:1***)
4. **Call on God's covenant name** (in Jesus' name)
5. **Let the fire fall**

## Jesus, the Baptizer With Fire

> *"He shall baptize you with the Holy Ghost, and with fire."*
> *(Matthew 3:11)*

John the Baptist knew: water was not enough.
We need **Spirit** and **fire**.

This fire is:

- **An inward branding** — marking you as God's own
- **A divine DNA injection** — changing your nature
- **A prophetic inheritance** — linking you to the fire-walkers of old

From Elijah to Jesus, from Pentecost to now — the fire is our signature of kingdom identity.


## Zion's Fire: Not Strange Fire

> *"There went out fire from the Lord, and devoured them..."*
> *(Leviticus 10:2)*

Nadab and Abihu brought **strange fire** — fire not authorised by God.
Many today burn with carnal fire, emotional zeal, or false doctrine.
But God responds only to the fire He starts.

> *"The fire on the altar shall be kindled by the priest, but it must come from heaven."*
> *(see Leviticus 9:24)*

Your role is to **prepare the altar**, not fake the flame.

## Seven Fire Altars in the Bible

| Altar | Fire Encounter | Meaning |
|---|---|---|
| Eden (Flaming Sword) | *Genesis 3:24* | Protection from unclean entry |
| Abraham's Altar | *Genesis 15:17* | Covenant & promise activation |
| Mount Sinai | *Exodus 19:18* | Fire of holiness & law |
| Tabernacle Fire | *Leviticus 9:24* | Acceptable worship |
| Elijah's Altar | *1 Kings 18:38* | Fire restores covenant order |
| Isaiah's Fire Coal | *Isaiah 6:6–7* | Fire purifies the mouth |
| Pentecost Fire | *Acts 2:3–4* | Fire releases boldness & Spirit-led utterance |

## Prophetic Call: Become an Altar of Fire

> *"Present your bodies a living sacrifice..."*
> *(Romans 12:1)*

You are not just a worshiper.
You are the altar.
You are the wood.
You are the sacrifice.
You are the flame-carrier.

Let the fire fall upon your altar — daily, continuously, eternally.

## Prophetic Decree:

O Lord, I yield myself as an altar of holy fire.
Burn away the strange fire, consume my flesh, and fill me with the fire of Your Spirit.
Let my prayers rise like incense.
Let my life burn with boldness.
Let Zion's flame never die in me."

In Jesus Christ's Might Name

*Amen*

# Chapter 17

## Strange Fire and Counterfeit Altars — The Spirit of Balaam vs. the Fire of God

*"There went out fire from the Lord, and devoured them, and they died before the Lord."*
*(Leviticus 10:2)*

*"Woe unto them! for they have gone in the way of Cain, and ran greedily after the error of Balaam for reward..."*
*(Jude 1:11)*

## What Is Strange Fire?

**Strange fire** is not just unauthorised fire — it is fire **born from the will of man, not the breath of God**.

- It imitates **true worship** but has no divine spark.
- It looks **powerful**, but carries no holiness.
- It burns **incense**, but not from a holy heart.

The sons of Aaron offered strange fire and **died instantly**. (**Leviticus 10:1–2**)

They brought fire **without permission**, without fear, and without a Word.

# The Spirit of Balaam: Prophet for Profit

Balaam is a key symbol of **religious corruption** in Scripture:

- **He heard from God** but **sold revelation for reward.**
- **He built altars** but **had no altar in his heart.**
- **He used enchantments** while pretending to be prophetic.
- He gave counsel that led Israel into **idolatry and immorality** (***Numbers 31:16***).

**Balaam offered sacrifices without fire from God.**
His fire was ambition, not anointing.

**False fire always follows the spirit of Balaam:**

- A platform without consecration
- A mouth full of blessings, but a heart full of compromise
- A sacrifice made to please men, not to honour God

# True Altars vs. Counterfeit Altars

| TRUE ALTAR (Zion) | COUNTERFEIT ALTAR (Balaam) |
| --- | --- |
| Fueled by obedience | Fueled by ambition |
| Fire from heaven | Fire from a strange source |
| Built by covenant | Built for crowd & money |
| Glory of God descends | Demonic deception ascends |
| Requires purity | Sells prophecy |
| Releases truth | Mixes truth with witchcraft |

# Cain, Balaam, and Korah — The Threefold Rebellion

*Jude 1:11* reveals three rebellion patterns:

1. **Cain** – offering without heart
2. **Balaam** – prophecy without purity
3. **Korah** – authority without submission

These three spirits still operate in churches:

- Strange fire in worship (**Cain**)
- Strange words in prophecy (**Balaam**)
- Strange order in leadership (**Korah**)

God never accepts an altar **not established by obedience.**

## The Fire Will Test Every Man's Work

> "Every man's work shall be made manifest: for the day shall declare it, because it shall be revealed by fire..."
> (1 Corinthians 3:13)

Fire reveals the origin.
God's fire will test:

- Your prayers
- Your revelations
- Your teachings
- Your altar

Only what was birthed in God will remain.

## The DNA of True Fire: The Spirit of Jesus

*"He shall baptize you with the Holy Ghost, and with fire."*
*(Matthew 3:11)*

- True fire comes from **the Word and Spirit together**.
- It will **purge**, **revive**, and **speak truth**.
- It burns out lies and awakens the dead.

Where there is no cross, there is strange fire.
Where there is no repentance, there is no flame.
Where there is no Holy Spirit, there is no altar.

## Signs of Strange Fire in the Church Today

- Emotional hype with no holiness
- Prophetic words mixed with manipulation
- Entertainment replacing intercession
- Motivational talk instead of sanctified truth
- Marketplace prophets chasing wealth over souls

If the altar is not based on **the Word, the Spirit, and the Cross**, it is **strange**.

## Zion's Call: Return to the True Altar

The Spirit of God is calling the remnant to return to the **altar of fire**:

- Lay down ambition.
- Cast out manipulation.
- Let God's fire fall on clean hearts again.

*"O Lord, let me not burn with strange fire.*
*Let Your flame purge my spirit.*
*Let my altar be acceptable to You."*

## Prophetic Declaration:

"I renounce the fire of Balaam, the counsel of deception, the altar of performance, and the corruption of false worship.
I choose the fire of Zion, the altar of Jesus Christ, and the purifying flame of the Holy Spirit.
Burn in me, O God, until only You remain!"

In Jesus Christ's Mighty Name. *Amen*

# Chapter 18

## The Fullness of God's Armour in One Body — Zion's Warrior Awakens

> *"For the weapons of our warfare are not carnal, but mighty through God to the pulling down of strong holds..."*
> *(2 Corinthians 10:4)*

> *"Put ye on the Lord Jesus Christ..."*
> *(Romans 13:14)*

## The Body as the Temple, the Armour as the Covering

> *"In that day will I raise up the tabernacle of David that is fallen..."*
> *(Amos 9:11)*

The full armour is also the **covering of the temple** — the remnant body rising as Zion.

- The **helmet** is the renewed mind of Christ.
- The **breastplate** is the indwelling of righteousness.
- The **shield** is unwavering trust in the Word.
- The **sword** is the activated Spirit-word in the mouth.
- The **loins girt** is pure holy marriage covenant and truth-tied identity.
- The **feet** are stability in the prophetic gospel of rest.

- **Prayer and bold utterance** are the incense and voice of the temple.

This is **not individual warfare alone**, but **a collective rise of a prophetic people** — Zion's Army.

## The Man of Fire — Warrior of Zion

> *"His body was like beryl, and his face as the appearance of lightning, and his eyes as lamps of fire…"*
> *(Daniel 10:6)*

The armour of God is also seen in prophetic visions:

- **Daniel saw a man clothed in fire and linen** — this is the image of spiritual warfare clothed in priesthood.
- **John saw Jesus with a sword coming from His mouth** — this is the Word awakened in judgment.

This is the man who **stands on the sea and the land** (*Revelation 10*). This is not just Jesus alone — this is **Christ in His Body**, the overcomers, **filled with the full measure of God** (*Ephesians 3:19*).

Zion's warrior is not just armoured — **He is flame-covered and Word-filled.**

## Overturn, Overturn, Until the Right One Comes

> *"I will overturn, overturn, overturn it: and it shall be no more, until he come whose right it is…"*
> *(Ezekiel 21:27)*

This is the warrior who:

- Bears all armour, not just pieces
- Walks in Christ, not just speaks about Him
- Overturns thrones, altars, and principalities
- Stands in the gap like the High Priest, and also rides like the Lion of Judah

The heavens have waited for this fullness — the armour becomes the **glory of God revealed in a body**.

## Flesh and Blood Cannot Inherit — But Spirit Man Will Rule

> *"Flesh and blood cannot inherit the kingdom…"*
> *(1 Corinthians 15:50)*

Satan, once a corrupted seed of light, fell and clothed himself in **fleshly kingdoms**. But the sons of light now come in **Spirit and fire**.

- Not by politics — but by prophecy.
- Not by title — but by testimony.
- Not by sword of iron — but by **the sword of the Spirit**.

# Final Awakening: The Man Clothed With the Fullness

> *"Awake, O Zion, put on thy strength, O Jerusalem; put on thy beautiful garments..."*
> *(Isaiah 52:1)*

The full armour is:

- The **mind** of the Spirit (helmet)
- The **heart** of righteousness (breastplate)
- The **loins girt** of truth (covenant)
- The **feet** of peace (path)
- The **hand** of faith (shield)
- The **mouth** of fire (sword)
- The **voice** of intercession (prayer)
- The **boldness** of Zion (utterance)

This is the army of light. This is **the man of *Revelation 12* — a woman clothed with the sun**, giving birth to the **male child clothed with armour**, who rules all nations with a rod of iron.

> *"And to her was granted that she should be arrayed in fine linen, clean and white: for the fine linen is the righteousness of saints."*
> *(Revelation 19:8)*

# Prophetic Charge

Clothe yourself, O warrior of Zion.
Let the full armour be your covenant mantle.
You are no longer just a man — you are a witness of glory,
a priest, a prophet, a king.
Let the Lord arise in you.
Let the armour breathe.
Let Christ fill your temple.

# Chapter 19

# Prayer for Nationalisation into the Kingdom of Heaven

Scriptural Foundation:

- *John 3:3* – "Jesus answered and said to him, 'Most assuredly, I say to you, unless one is born again, he cannot see the kingdom of God.'"

- *Philippians 3:20* – "For our citizenship is in heaven, from which we also eagerly wait for the Savior, the Lord Jesus Christ."

- *Ephesians 2:19* – "Now therefore you are no longer strangers and foreigners, but fellow citizens with the saints and members of the household of God."

- *Colossians 1:13* – "He has delivered us from the power of darkness and conveyed us into the kingdom of the Son of His love."

- *Romans 10:9* – "That if you confess with your mouth the Lord Jesus and believe in your heart that God has raised Him from the dead, you will be saved."

**Righteous Judge of Heaven and Earth,**

I come before Your throne, the **throne of Grace** in **the Court of Heaven**, in the name of Jesus Christ, my Lord and Saviour. I stand by the power of His precious blood, which has **redeemed me** and **bought my salvation**. I come humbly and boldly, desiring to be **nationalised** into the Kingdom of Heaven—to become a **true citizen of Your heavenly realm**.

**Father**, Your Word declares in ***John 3:3*** that **unless one is born again**, they cannot see the Kingdom of God. Today, **I renounce any citizenship** I once held in this world and any **ties to the powers of darkness**. I acknowledge that I have been **transferred from the kingdom of darkness into the Kingdom of the Son** of Your love (***Colossians 1:13***). I declare that I am no longer a stranger or foreigner, but a **fellow citizen with the saints** and a member of the household of God (***Ephesians 2:19***).

**Lord Jesus**, I believe with all my heart that You are the **Son of the living God**, that You died for my sins and rose again to grant me eternal life (**Romans 10:9**). I now receive You as my **personal Saviour, my Redeemer, the only Way, the Truth,** and **the Life**. You are the **Door to the Father's heart** and the only **path to salvation**. I do not want to **perish** with the world, but to **live eternally with You**.

At this moment, I **[Your Full Name]** solemnly, sincerely, and truthfully affirm my love, my seriousness, and my desire to follow You and serve You in **holiness and righteousness**. I pledge my full allegiance to You, O King of kings and Lord of lords. I give my loyalty to the third Heaven and honour its **rights and freedoms**. I desire to settle with You, **Lord Jesus**. I repent of the way I have **lived my life and of all my sins**. Take over **my heart and my destiny**. Save me, cleanse me, and change me.

I beseech that You **seal my heavenly citizenship today**. Let the record of **my new identity** be **registered in the Court of Heaven**. Write my name in the **Lamb's Book of Life**, and erase it from the **book of death and judgment**. Let every **legal claim the enemy** has over my past be **cancelled** and **rendered powerless by the blood of Jesus**.

**Lord**, I am ready to walk the path of **righteousness and holiness**. I cast all **my cares and all of myself upon You**, for You care for me and loved me and laid Your life as the Lamb slain from **the foundation of the world**. Let Your **will be done** in my life as it is in Heaven.

By Your blood, I now receive eternal life. I proclaim that I am a **new creature**. By the word of Your testimony, I am made free indeed. **Fill me and baptize me** with the **Holy Ghost and fire**. Thank You, Lord Jesus, for giving me the right and the power to become a child of God, born **not of flesh but of the Spirit**, according to **the new covenant sealed in Your blood**.

I believe **You died** for me, and on the **third day**, You rose again. You are now seated at the right hand of the **Father in glory**, and I receive You as the Lord of my life. Through You, I have **received grace, peace, forgiveness, and eternal inheritance**. I stand holy, blameless, and without fault before the **Court of Heaven** because of the **righteousness imputed to me through Your sacrifice**.

Now, I **declare that the power of sin, death, and Satan—including the grave—has been broken over my life**. I walk in the eternal victory of the Cross. From this day forward, I will never look back. Backward—never. Forward—forever.

**Degree and Declare**: I am a citizen of Heaven. I live for Your Kingdom. **I walk in Your authority and power.** I receive the **full inheritance of health, peace, righteousness, Wealth, and provision, even eternal life.**

In Jesus' mighty name, I pray.

*Amen.*

# *EPILOGUE*

Every book written in the Spirit is more than ink on pages — it is a witness in eternity, a stone of remembrance, and a seed planted in Zion. This work, *Oracles of Faith*, is not merely a record of revelation but a covenant scroll — birthed in prayer, sealed in fire, and aligned with the testimony of Jesus Christ.

We stand in an hour where darkness intensifies, yet the light of the Spirit shines brighter. Faith, in its purest form, is not passive belief but the living voice of God echoing through His people. These oracles are not to be admired from a distance, but to be embodied, spoken, and lived — for the Word becomes flesh in every generation that yields to the Spirit.

As this book closes, the scroll in heaven remains open. The oracles continue to flow to those who hunger and thirst for righteousness. May every reader who encounters these words rise as a living testimony — a priest of the Sabbath, a vessel of the Spirit, and a voice of Zion in these last days.

The final word is not the end but the beginning. For in every oracle, eternity breathes, and in every declaration, the Spirit of Truth prepares a bride made ready.

**So let it be written. So let it be sealed. So let it be done.**

— *Anthony Mwangi* — *the BRANCH seated in Zion*

# AFTERWORD

As these pages close, the Spirit whispers that the journey has only just begun. What has been written here is not an end, but a gateway—an invitation into the living fire of truth. These words are not merely for study, but for witness; not only for the mind, but for the soul and body to be aligned with the Spirit of God.

Every chapter, every revelation, every altar declaration was forged in prayer and sealed in the court of heaven. They are not mine—they belong to the Eternal Spirit who breathes through all creation. I have been but a vessel, a pen dipped in fire, set to trace the mysteries hidden before the foundation of the world.

May this book remain a living stone within Zion, calling forth the remnant, stirring holy remembrance, and restoring the order of Sabbath in the last days. And may all who read it walk boldly as witnesses of the covenant, clothed in the full armour of God, ready to stand until the final trumpet sounds.

The Spirit and the Bride say, *Come.*

**—Anthony Mwangi, the BRANCH seated in Zion**

# ACKNOWLEDGEMENT

I bow in reverence to the Eternal Spirit—the Holy One—who is the breath behind every word in this book. Without His light, no truth could be seen; without His fire, no revelation could burn. To the Spirit of the Lord, the Spirit of Wisdom, Understanding, Counsel, Might, Knowledge, and the Fear of the Lord, be all glory forever.

I honour Jesus Christ, the Living Word and the Stone of Fire, whose blood speaks better things and whose covenant has sealed this work in eternity.

I acknowledge my beloved family, who have carried me in prayer and stood with me through the travail of writing. To my wife, whose vision and intercession have been a lamp in the night seasons, and to my household, who have endured the fire of this calling—I honour you deeply.

I thank every intercessor, every prophetic voice, and every kingdom labourer who has walked with me in silence, sacrifice, and faith. Your unseen prayers are written in heaven as pillars of this work.

Finally, to the remnant of Zion—those called to rise in these last days—this book is for you. May you read not only with eyes, but with spirit; may you receive not only with understanding, but with fire.

All glory belongs to the One seated on the Throne.

**—Anthony Mwangi, the BRANCH seated in Zion**

www.ingramcontent.com/pod-product-compliance
Lightning Source LLC
Chambersburg PA
CBHW041619220426
43661CB00046B/1504